19

MW01140626

Chrome

Is Where the Heart Is

Order this book online at www.trafford.com/07-1518
or email orders@trafford.com

Most Trafford titles are also available at major online book retailers.

Note for Librarians: A cataloguing record for this book is available from Library
and Archives Canada at www.collectionscanada.ca/amicus/index-e.html

Printed in Victoria, BC, Canada.

ISBN: 978-1-4251-3810-3

*We at Trafford believe that it is the responsibility of us all, as both individuals
and corporations, to make choices that are environmentally and socially sound.
You, in turn, are supporting this responsible conduct each time you purchase a
Trafford book, or make use of our publishing services. To find out how you are
helping, please visit www.trafford.com/responsiblepublishing.html*

*Our mission is to efficiently provide the world's finest, most comprehensive
book publishing service, enabling every author to experience success.
To find out how to publish your book, your way, and have it available
worldwide, visit us online at www.trafford.com/10510*

 www.trafford.com

North America & international
toll-free: 1 888 232 4444 (USA & Canada)
phone: 250 383 6864 ♦ fax: 250 383 6804 ♦ email: info@trafford.com

The United Kingdom & Europe
phone: +44 (0)1865 722 113 ♦ local rate: 0845 230 9601
facsimile: +44 (0)1865 722 868 ♦ email: info.uk@trafford.com

10 9 8 7 6 5

Acknowledgments

There is a very special group of people who have played a significant role in making *Chrome Is Where the Heart Is* a reality. A special thanks to all three of our children, Kevin, Mark and Kristen, who have been there for so many of the chapters. Thanks Mark, for the enthusiastic bug collection! Thank you, Kevin, for your rendition of one of my favorite cars, the 1955 Olds that is parked on the front cover. So cool! Thanks also to Dave Marty at Soundview Design for the awesome job with the cover layout! A special thanks to Karen Parkin, my editor, for all of your tireless energy and enthusiastic support! I appreciate it so much! Thanks to Vanessa and Leanne at Trafford Publishing for your guidance in pulling this whole project together. And finally, a great big thank you to Annie for sticking beside me through this entire journey! Thanks again to each and every one of you for the polish and shine that you have brought to this "chrome." I can see each of your reflections as I admire this finished work. What a team. What an adventure. What a memory. Thank you all from the very bottom of my heart.

Dedication

This book is dedicated to the three favorite girls in my life: Annie, my sweetheart.

You are my best friend, lover, and soul matey. Our journey together has taken us a lot of places and it is so good to have shared them all with you. I'm still crazy about you after all these years and I'm excited about the road that stretches out before us.

Kristen, my "little girl."

You have filled my heart with love and so much happiness. Thanks for your sunny smile and for always believing in me. What a blessing you are, and I am so proud to be your dad.

Grandma Davis, Joan, Annie's mom, and one of my greatest fans.

You have been a true inspiration for this project from the start. Your encouragement and support are priceless. Thanks for being you.

Contents

Introduction

If any of us tried to remember our first word, chances are we would draw a blank. We have to rely on our parents, who were there and fondly remember that day, that time, that word. For many, those first words were probably "Mama" or "Dada." But this wasn't the case for me. My parents told me that my first word was "Adillac," and I have had a passion for cars ever since.

I realized I was hopelessly in love with cars when I went car shopping in the dead of winter. I trudged around a car lot and wondered why none of the salesmen were coming out to greet me. In fact, they seemed to be sneering at me from inside their nice, warm office. Then it hit me. All the cars on the lot looked identical. They were all the same color. They were all covered with four inches of fresh snow. I decided to hold off my search until the spring.

While most of us might not remember our first *words*, I'll bet that all of us can remember our first *cars*. The make, the year, the color. It is all right there. As we take a little time to look back at that time in our lives, the memories begin to fill our minds and maybe even our hearts. Think of the friends you had then and the experiences you shared. Maybe you remember your second car. And your third. Or perhaps, like me, you remember all the vehicles you've owned and have attached distinct and fond memories to each one.

In fact, I've taken some time to look back and remember not only my first car but also the twenty-seven vehicles that have followed it, weaving their way through my life and experiences. Now I invite you to ride along with me and journey to the past. Every word and every story here is true, and if you have even *half* the fun reading it as I have had writing it I will have accomplished my goal.

It's all about taking the time to look back, linger, and let the warmth of these memories fill your heart and touch your funny bone. What's more, it might even take you back to those times, those places, those cars in your own life, spinning a tale from the fabric of your memories. It's all about life, about love, about who we are and where we've been. All roads lead home, because *Chrome Is Where the Heart Is.*

BOB BELL

1.

The Firemen

One of the best things about growing up in a small town in the fifties was the volunteer fire department. Our local fire station was an all-volunteer effort and was located smack-dab in the middle of Alderwood Manor, about twenty miles north of Seattle. On top of the fire station sat a great big siren that could be heard for miles. Whenever there was a fire, the siren wailed and the firemen, wherever they were, would grab their gear, jump in their cars, and hightail it for the fire station. Each of them had a blue light mounted on the front of his car, which (I was positive as an eight year old) was his license to drive as fast as he could and take any corner on two wheels. In my mind those blue lights transformed the oldest jalopy into the fastest race car in the county. I dreamed that I too would some day have a blue light on my car.

THE PLAYERS

In those days, volunteer firemen had their "day jobs" too, but after hours they were on call 24/7. My dad, Jim, worked in a dairy during the day. But on evenings and weekends, in my book, he was the coolest fireman ever. And his red and white 1957 Ford pickup—complete with the wraparound rear window—appeared pretty impressive with that blue light mounted in the grill. It may have actually looked like a dirty old Ford truck on the outside, but I was sure that underneath beat the heart of a hot rod as I saw Dad lay a patch of rubber a few times (with the help of a little gravel in the right places).

Volunteer firefighting was serious business, so Dad would always back his truck into the driveway (he even left his keys in the ignition) for a quick exit should duty call. And he always hung his boots, pants, coat, and fire helmet by the front door, ready to grab as he raced out.

The absolute best place to be when the fire siren sounded was right there at the station. That was the heart of the action, not to mention the best vantage point to see the handful of volunteers come sliding into the parking lot from every direction. They would jump out of their cars and onto the old red Kenworth fire engine then roar off to the fire—siren screeching and red lights flashing. Remember, this was the fifties and there were no pulsating strobe lights—just the big red revolving light on the cab and the blinking lights on the back.

The chances of being downtown near the station at the same time the fire siren blew were about as remote as sitting next to the fireplace when Santa came down the chimney. So, the next best place to be was at home on 33rd Avenue—*my* street. We were lucky enough to have *four* volunteer firemen in our neighborhood. We lived on one side of 33rd Avenue (it was gravel in those days), and Stan, Ray, and Dick, the other volunteer firemen, lived on the other side. Nobody ever heard of carpooling in the fifties, so when the fire siren blew each of them would jump into his car for the race to the station. The thrill for us kids was to watch and see whose dad would be the first one out of the driveway. What could be cooler than that for a kid who loved cars? To me, the race to the station had to be better, or at least as good as, the start of the Indy 500.

Of all the firemen on 33rd Avenue, Stan was the hippest, with his flat-top haircut and turquoise 1955 Ford Ranch Wagon with dual exhausts that sounded like a real hot rod. (How many times had I hoped against hope that Dad would someday get dual exhausts on his '57 Ford pickup?) Next door to Stan lived Ray, who, with his wife Margaret, had a lot of kids and drove a two-tone 1952 Lincoln sedan. Next door to Ray, directly across the street from our house, was where Dick lived. From my perspective, Dick seemed different from the rest of the firemen. Not a weird kind of different, but just different. Dick was a great big man, the others were average size. Dick never hurried, while the other three never seemed to slow down. His old red 1949 Pontiac "Silver Streak" seemed to crawl out of the driveway at a snail's pace. I don't know which was bigger, Dick's waistline or that Pontiac's engine, but they made quite a pair and could always be counted on for last place out of the driveway and down to the station. The dust that had been kicked up by the other three firemen had already settled by the time the old Pontiac sputtered down the road. And it wouldn't have mattered much if Dick always arrived at the fire station dead last, except that he was the one who drove the fire truck!

ON YOUR MARK, GET SET

One warm summer afternoon a bunch of the neighborhood kids sat in our yard licking ice-cold Popsicles that my dad had brought home from the dairy. The lazy summer calm was suddenly shattered by the shrill call of the fire siren, alerting the firemen of a pending emergency.

"Gentlemen, start your engines."

We ran down to the end of the driveway where the best view of the street was by our picket fence. (I had painstakingly labored over that fence when Dad decided that it needed to be painted white instead of green. Ugh! My vote would have been to leave it green or tear it down, but nobody in my family had bothered to ask for my opinion.)

A commotion stirred up at all four houses as these brave firemen scrambled for their gear and ran for their cars in a mad dash to reach the station. I heard Dad's Ford pickup first and looked around to see him shooting out of the driveway in his blue-light special. He even spun the rear tires right there in front of me as he roared into the street. What a moment to savor for this kid!

But wait. There was thunder at Stan's house across the street as the '55 Ford Ranch Wagon lurched out of the driveway and into the street just ahead of Dad. The dust was kicking up pretty good by the time Ray fired up that old Lincoln and barreled out of his driveway, throwing gravel in every direction.

The two Fords and the Lincoln raced down the street and disappeared around the corner, giving us kids the signal that it was time to resume our Popsicle break. I glanced across the street just in time to see Dick's Pontiac turn out of his driveway and head for the fire station. I often wondered if the others might have mistakenly thought that Dick was already waiting for them at the station or, worse yet, gone ahead to the fire without them.

The years have flown by and though Dad, Stan, Ray, and Dick are long gone, they live on in my memories. They were heroes to me, and to all of the kids on 33rd Avenue. I will forever admire their commitment to serve others and make our community safer—blue lights and all.

What I liked: My dad was my hero.

What I learned: It's not always important to be first.

BOB BELL

2.

Two Wheelin'

Because my love for automobiles started at a very young age, playing with toy cars was my favorite pastime. I can well remember going to the local Ben Franklin store on a Saturday afternoon with my allowance in hand in search of another toy car. While my older brother, Scott, would spend his time looking at airplanes and army men on the next aisle over, I would be in heaven looking at the cars on aisle three. The cheaper toy cars were made of plastic, but for a few cents more you could get a metal car with a friction motor that made an authentic engine sound (or so it seemed to this kid).

One Christmas morning when I was about seven years old, I awoke feeling very cheated after hearing Scott's tale of how he had heard Santa's sled on the roof and had actually seen the headlights from the sleigh shining on the garage door.

When we finally got the green light to come downstairs, we raced to see what Santa had left us. Mom's aluminum tree with red balls and revolving color wheel made a dazzling backdrop for what was parked in the middle of the living room: not one but two glistening bicycles! As our parents looked on proudly, Scott made his way to the black-and-silver three-speed English Racer while I was totally taken with a shiny red Schwinn Typhoon. I just couldn't believe this beautiful new bicycle was my very own!

Still in my pajamas and slippers, I excitedly hopped up on my new set of wheels. With the kickstand down, I could stand right up on the pedals, pretending to make the final lap of the Daytona 500 stock car race. There I was, barreling down the final stretch toward the checkered flag with victory only seconds away. I was in absolute ecstasy! My glee was short lived, however, as I came to the grim realization that terry cloth bedroom slippers aren't the recommended footwear for Daytona drivers on bicycles. Thank goodness at that moment Mom wasn't busy snapping pictures with her old box camera. It was probably the first Daytona crash to involve only the driver and not the "car." As my slippers slid off the pedals, I crashed down on that straight bar in the middle that defines a boy's bike from the rest. I straddled that bar and took the full impact right between my legs. I'm sure that race car drivers must wear some kind of protection to prevent such hostile blows, but here I was in nothing but my pajamas with nothing else to cushion the impact. I let out a blood curdling scream of pain as Scott looked on, amused to see his little brother in such a predicament. My voice changed that morning—not deeper, as when boys begin to approach adolescence, but rather a few notes higher, even after the pain subsided.

BOB BELL

CRUISIN' AND SCHMOOZIN'

I eventually recovered with apparently no lasting damage and spent many long summer days riding up and down our street, lost in my world of make-believe and often pretending (you guessed it) that I was driving a car of some kind. Our street was my highway, raceway, and getaway. Sometimes I would pedal fast, racing at Daytona or the Indy 500; at other times I'd cruise, taking a Sunday drive with my convertible top down.

When Dad's friend George Bowman and his wife would come for a visit, they would drive up in their sparkling 1957 Ford Country Sedan station wagon. I was convinced that Mr. Bowman washed and waxed his car every day of the week. This pastel green and white beauty sported a shiny chrome luggage rack on top. For days after a visit from the Bowmans, I would ride up and down our street behind the wheel of my very own 1957 pastel green and white Ford Country Sedan station wagon, cleverly disguised as a red Schwinn Typhoon.

Another one of Dad's lifelong buddies, Grant, was a Ford man just like my dad was. Grant and his wife, Marguerite, lived in the eastern part of the state, so we didn't see them often. Having a thing for turquoise cars, Grant would always drive up in a late model Ford, each one dressed in some kind of turquoise and white paint scheme. My favorite was his 1959 Ford sedan. He replaced that one a few years later with a solid turquoise 1963 Ford Galaxy and then four years later with another Galaxy, this time a 1967 turquoise model with a white vinyl top. I dreamed of moving in with them and washing their cars for my room and board. I spent many long summer afternoons cruising up and down our street, behind the wheel of one of Grant's fine cars, once again disguised as a red Schwinn Typhoon. It was heaven on wheels, or so it seemed to this chrome-loving youngster.

SUNDAY SURPRISE

My parents were both active members in our local community church. While Mom sewed blankets for the missionaries and worked in the church kitchen, Dad's chosen place of service was outside in the parking lot. Dad was really practical like that, and for as long as I can remember he was there every Sunday morning, directing traffic and helping folks find a place to park. He would recruit Scott and me to help him on those big Sundays—like Easter—when the pasture in back of the church doubled as an extra parking lot. We rose to the occasion and enjoyed watching the ladies in their finest Easter dresses and hats stepping through the muddy pasture to the church. I chuckled to myself as I could picture any one of them stepping in a pile of old cow poop as they hurried into the church service. Dad ran a smooth operation, greeting everyone with a warm smile and cheery "Good morning!" as he pointed them to the desired parking area.

One Sunday morning I decided to ride my red Schwinn bicycle to church, just a couple of blocks from our house. When I pulled in, Dad was already there directing traffic, so I proudly parked my bike right next to his red '57 Ford pickup truck, which was backed in the last row by the street. As I walked up to the old church, I kept looking over my shoulder at my bike: that day it was a fancy red roadster and seemed to beckon me to come and take it out on the racetrack. Certain of the wrath I would incur if I decided to skip Sunday school, I delayed my racing plans until after church was over.

The minute Sunday school ended, I sprinted to the parking lot to my imaginary race car as if it were the start of the Indy 500. Halfway there I stopped dead in my tracks. Dad's Ford was still there, but my red Schwinn was gone! I ran to the scene of the crime and stared in disbelief, launching into a verbal tirade laced with profanities, promptly forgetting the morning Bible lesson. Dad heard me and came running across the parking lot, dodging cars and people. He was especially kind to me that Sunday morning and resisted the urge—at least outwardly—to tell me how stupid it was to leave my bike by the side of the road.

By late afternoon the mystery was half solved when we discovered my bike frame at a Salvation Army drop-off box. No wheels, handlebars, or seat, just the frame. Dad assured me that my Schwinn could be as good as new after some new wheels and such. Sure enough, it wasn't more than a week later (and a couple of trips to the bicycle store) that my Schwinn Typhoon was ready to roll. Life was good, and I felt like I was on top of the world as I cruised up and down our street once again.

FLAT TUESDAY

It was summertime and the long warm days were great for doing all the things that ten-year-old boys do. Most days would find me on my bicycle, cruising up and down 33rd Avenue with all the neighborhood kids. Our days were full and running over with make-believe, fun, and adventure.

One particularly hot Tuesday afternoon I decided to favor the little Thomas kids next door with a visit to their lemonade stand. I had been riding a lot that day— pretending my bicycle was once again something other than a Schwinn Typhoon. I pulled into the Thomas's driveway and parked my rig directly behind their rig, a 1956 dark green Ford station wagon.

The Thomas boys, thrilled at the prospect of a customer, smiled big as I approached for what was undoubtedly going to be a really big sale. I looked over their little handmade sign that read "fresh lemonade for a nickel." As their eyes danced with glee over their pending sale, I reached deep in my pocket for some change. "Well guys," I said sternly, "how about two cups for a quarter?" I'm pretty sure that by this time the Thomas boys would have sold me the whole stand and thrown in their little sister, Amy, for a quarter as they excitedly poured me two tiny paper cups of their cherished brew.

Speaking of Amy, where was she in all of this action? It was then that I noticed the green Ford had started to roll backward down the driveway. Panic struck as I dropped my cup and raced over to rescue my Schwinn Typhoon. I mean, who cared about the Thomas's station wagon? I reached the back of the car and tried to stop it, not realizing that the laws of physics were not going to work to the advantage of this ten year old trying to stop a 5,000-pound Ford wagon. I watched in horror as the rolling Ford consumed my Schwinn at one end and spit it out of the other, then continued out into the street. Mrs. Thomas appeared out of nowhere, jumped in the car, and stopped it in the street before it had a chance to do any more damage. My Schwinn Typhoon, which only a few months earlier had been stolen and stripped by thieves, now lay flat as a pancake in the Thomas's driveway. Sweet little Amy had wandered over, slipped into the car unnoticed, and released the brake to do a little cruising herself. So it was back to the bicycle store, this time with some of the Thomas's money, for another round of parts and

BOB BELL

a second rebuild. In just two weeks I was back in business.

I eventually outgrew the Schwinn and joined the Sting-Ray bicycle craze—with the banana seat and high-rise handlebars. In the coming months I became the proud owner of not one but two Sting-Rays, one built from the ground up and the other purchased brand new from my paper-route earnings. They both served me well until I began to notice girls in a whole new light. It wasn't long after my first kiss when I determined that, among other things, it was time to move up from two wheels to four.

What I liked: Riding along in my own little world of make-believe.

What I learned: Race car drivers should never wear bedroom slippers on the track.

3.

First Drives

Think back to those times in your childhood when you had that magical opportunity to drive a real car for fun. For as long as I can remember, I dreamed of that day, but I knew that, barring a miracle, it would never happen in my family until I turned sixteen, which seemed light years away. After all, I was sure by this time in my life that my parents' favorite word was no. I chose instead to dream of that day when I could really drive, and then one very hot summer afternoon when I was ten years old, in Nebraska of all places, my dream came true, my ship came in big time, and I remember it like it was yesterday.

TWISTIN' WITH THE TWINS

The year was 1962 and the Seattle world's fair was in full swing. That summer, while folks from all over the country traveled to Seattle for the fair, my family visited my mom's side of the family in the little town of Valentine, Nebraska. Her niece and family, the McCrays, lived on a sprawling ranch at the edge of town. They had three girls: one who was five years older than me and thirteen-year-old twins. At the McCray's ranch we could ride their Shetland pony and listen to a cool old jukebox in the basement: It played three songs for a quarter, and as soon as the music started playing you could open the door and get your quarter back. Best of all, I learned to do the twist for the very first time.

"Just pretend that you're putting out a cigarette with your foot and move to the music" was all the instruction that I needed from Dede and Donnie (short for Deatrice and Donna), those cute thirteen-year-old twins. What a blast! But when I was presented with the prospect of actually driving Auntie Ethel's 1951 Packard sedan, I ditched the dancing in a hurry.

Auntie Ethel was Mom's older sister who had passed away a few years before, and her old Packard still sat at the McCray ranch. The long dirt driveway ran from the main road, down around the house, and to the barn, providing ample room to drive the old car. Who in the world would choose to ride a Shetland pony when they could drive a Packard? What a thrill it was to get behind the wheel and wile away the afternoon driving up and down the long dirt driveway. My twelve-year-old brother, Scott, wasn't interested in the least: the twins, not the car, captured his undivided attention. But for me, driving the old Packard was a new-found freedom that my parents didn't seem to mind at all.

To them it was harmless fun, but for me it was the absolute highlight of the summer, even topping the opportunity to twist with a couple of teenage girls. Ah, the memories!

FOURTEEN AND LOTS TO CHAUFFER IT

After the mountaintop driving experience in Nebraska (where there are no mountains!), there came a long dry spell, and I had resigned myself to having to wait until I was sixteen to drive again. Meanwhile, I dreamed of the Nebraska twins and pondered why in the world I had chosen to spend more time with a 1951 Packard than with the world's cutest twin girls who dared to teach me the twist. Maybe Scott wasn't so dumb after all. I was fourteen when another golden driving opportunity dropped right into my lap.

Our family was visiting my Uncle Van and Auntie Mildred in the town of Yakima, Washington. There wasn't a whole lot to do short of sitting around and listening to grown-ups talk.

One long, lazy afternoon I found myself sitting in the driver's seat of Uncle Van's 1967 Dodge Monaco, listening to the radio. I was daydreaming as usual, most likely wishing that I could be twisting my way through the Midwest with the twins, who were now undoubtedly cuter than ever. I didn't see my Uncle Van approaching, so when he opened the passenger door he startled me right out of my daydreaming.

"Hey, Bobbie!" he greeted enthusiastically. "Let's go for a ride downtown." (Uncle Van was one of the few people who called me Bobbie and had done so ever since I could remember. While I didn't like *just anyone* calling me Bobbie, it sounded okay coming from Uncle Van. And besides, it was a whole lot better than some of the names my brother used for me.)

"Sure," I mumbled, reaching for the door handle to get out and move around to the passenger side.

"No! Stay there!" Uncle Van ordered. "Why don't you drive?"

I was shocked, and confusion was probably written all over my face.

"Me?" I asked, as if there were ten of us in the car. "I'm only fourt—"

"Oh, you'll be fine, Bobbie," he said assuredly, closing the door. "Go ahead and start the engine. I have a doctor's appointment downtown and we need to be there in ten minutes."

My heart was pounding as I proudly accepted this challenge, turning the key and hearing the big 318 roar to life under the hood.

Totally relaxed, Uncle Van casually rattled off the directions as I navigated the busy streets of downtown Yakima. When we arrived at the doctor's office, he got out of the car and told me he'd be back in a few minutes. I opted to stay put: I was in heaven and didn't want the dream to end.

After a few minutes Uncle Van emerged from the doctor's office and took his co-pilot position in the passenger seat.

"Okay, Bobbie!" he said gleefully. "Take us back to the house."

"I'll do my best," I croaked, feigning confidence. Despite a throat as dry as dust and fingers clenched stiff, I was determined to savor every second behind the wheel of the big red Dodge. I turned the key and the engine once again roared to life.

We made it all the way back to the house without hitting anybody or being stopped by the police. I even brought the car to a safe stop right next to the curb, exactly where I had been sitting less than an hour before.

"Great job, Bobbie!" Uncle Van smiled as he patted my

shoulder. I was convinced that once my uncle reported to my folks what an excellent driver I was, they would be thrilled about this good news and ask me to do all of the driving in the family from that day forward. But reality set in when we walked in the house and my mom heard about the drive downtown. It was only June, but let me tell you fireworks were going off right there in Yakima in broad daylight that afternoon. I hadn't seen my mom that mad since the day my friend Dickie and I "borrowed" a dozen eggs from the old neighborhood chicken rancher and smashed them one by one on the shed wall.

What to do now? My dad had impressed upon me years earlier that it was never a good idea to pout or throw a tantrum, so I had to suck it up and wait for the hollering to stop. Keeping my head down and eyes riveted to the floor, I held on to the wonderful memory of how fun that drive had been. Dad in his infinite wisdom chose not to say much, and once Mom stepped off her soap box I glanced up at Uncle Van across the room. When he flashed me a big smile and winked, I realized that I would probably survive.

ANOTHER DAY, ANOTHER DODGE

After another year and a half crawled by I was finally able to get my learner's permit, which qualified me to enroll in driver's education class—one of those rites of passage that comes with high school. There is a real feeling of "having arrived" when it comes to the actual drive-time portion of the class. I was pleased to be assigned to a car with two cute girls as my driving partners. By age fifteen-and-a-half, I had come to realize that there were cute girls everywhere! We had a great time taking turns driving all over town with Mr. Hubbard, our no-nonsense driving instructor. He never smiled very much, but was one of the most patient men I had ever met.

Our driver's ed car was a 1968 Dodge station wagon, an enormous vehicle with loads of power. This wagon was so huge that the girls had a tough time trying to parallel park it. I was smart enough to not snicker as the girls tried over and over again to maneuver that thing between two orange safety cones. I did my best to support and encourage them.

When my turn came around, I was fortunate to get it right the first time. This move not only scored high marks with Mr. Hubbard but also seemed to momentarily impress the girls (although they weren't asking me for my phone number or joining me for lunch in the cafeteria).

But, as my dad used to remind me, "What goes around comes around," which is precisely what happened the day I took my driver's license test. I had sailed through the written test, which only served to increase my confidence for the driving test.

On the Saturday morning I was scheduled to take my test, the licensing facility was packed with eager new drivers and their tired parents who just stood around wondering how their babies could possibly be old enough to drive. At this particular facility, every potential driver performed the parallel parking portion of the test right there in front of God, the other young drivers, all of our parents, and anyone else who happened to pass by. The task was to drive up to the curb and then back into the parking slot between four orange cones, just as we had done a million times in driver's ed.

When my turn came, the policeman administering the driver's

BOB BELL

test instructed me to parallel park. And right there, in front of a sea of witnesses, I proceeded to back up onto the curb—not once but twice—then knock down three out of the four orange cones. I tried again and then again, until he scribbled a note on his clipboard and directed me to continue with the test. Humiliated, I realized we hadn't even left the parking lot.

My next blunder was at an intersection. He asked me to turn right. I then proceeded to turn on the left blinker and turn left. Halfway through the intersection he blurted, "You're not turning right!"

"No," I replied, trying to keep my wits together, "I'm turning left."

Just as I realized my error, he scribbled another note on his clipboard.

"Sorry," I said, attempting damage control. "I messed up." I sensed that this brilliant comment probably sealed my doom.

As he jotted more notes on his clipboard, I was sure that I had failed miserably. He guided me back to the department of licensing and told me to park the car and turn off the engine.

"Congratulations!" he said heartily, smiling for the first time. "You passed! You might want to work on your parallel parking a little, but outside of that you did fine."

"Thanks very much!" I replied, breathing a huge sigh of relief and secretly hoping that the two young ladies from my driver's ed car might give me another look now that I had my license. What a dreamer.

At age sixteen I felt on top of the world. One of my two dreams had come true. I was now a legal driver with my very own driver's license. Now all I needed was a car. I smiled as I thought about the Nebraska Packard and my joy ride through the streets of Yakima in Uncle Van's Dodge Monaco. That seemed like kid stuff now. At age sixteen, life was good and getting better by the minute.

What I liked: Four wheels are a whole lot more fun than two.

What I learned: Whenever the opportunity comes to dance— take it.

4.

The One that Got Away

One of the most exciting times of my life was when my parents gave me the "green light" to buy my first car. By age sixteen I had saved up a whopping $300 in paper-route and lawn-mowing earnings—now I was ready to deal.

Some of my friends had already purchased their first cars. My friend Jerry was especially proud of his 1959 Chevy Impala. It was a washed-out yellow color with green vinyl interior. Jerry purchased it with a good-sized hole in the windshield and the lingering odor of the pasture it had sat in for months. A new windshield took care of the hole, but that musty field smell lasted a lifetime.

THE SHORT LIST

After carefully combing the classifieds, I had found two cars that were "lookers" in my book. The first was a pink and white 1957 Pontiac four-door sedan with a $135 price tag. The second was a 1959 Chevy Impala, yes, the same make and model as Jerry's, but I was convinced—after reading the advertisement—that this one hands down was going to be way better.

When Dad agreed to take me out to look over these two exciting prospects, I practically turned cartwheels in the front yard. We stopped and looked at the Pontiac first. It was obvious that the owner had taken great care of the car: There were no dents, rust, or cracked glass, and the upholstery was perfect. The tires were good. I was convinced that I had never set my eyes on anything so beautiful.

"Mr. Pontiac" must have either liked me or felt sorry for me as he watched me lovingly drool over this gorgeous car. "Well, sonny," he smiled, "I can tell you like the car, and knowing that it would be your first car, I'll let you have it for $100."

My heart skipped a beat. One hundred bucks and it would be mine! I would even have $200 left in the bank to fix it up, buy some fancy wheels or maybe a big stereo. I was ready to say "sold" and shake on it when my heart skipped another beat. I stared in disbelief, unable to grasp the cold hard reality that there was a serious flaw in this otherwise pristine piece of automotive excellence: the Pontiac didn't have license plates. What could be worse than this? I mean, the car might as well have been sitting there without an engine or seats.

Mr. Pontiac picked right up on my crestfallen look, which wasn't too hard as I stood there ready to start bawling. "Not a problem, sonny, you can get a new set of plates at the department of licensing."

"Is he absolutely nuts?" I asked myself. "Doesn't he know that I want to drive this baby home tonight?" This was certainly no way to treat a first-time car buyer who had access to 300 bucks. "Besides," I continued to mope to myself, "I can't wait around all summer for plates. No wonder he is willing to 'let it go' for $100." It even occurred to me that maybe Mr. Pontiac should offer to pay me $100 to take this crate off his hands. I chose not to disclose my thoughts as I stood there fighting back the tears.

I decided to break the silence and take control of this already-tense situation. "It definitely is a nice car and I'd like to think it over," I said, trying to sound mature. Secretly I hoped that Mr. Pontiac would come to my rescue and say something like, "Wait! I do have the new plates and I was just getting ready to put them on when you drove up."

We stood there awkwardly for a moment or two and then I looked at Dad. "We'll think it over and get back with you," he said, looking at me as he turned to leave.

"Thank you," I said, forcing myself to smile as I shook Mr. Pontiac's hand. "That sure is a beautiful car." I turned to leave and never went back.

What I liked: Everything about that '57 Pontiac, plates or no plates.

What I learned: If you love something, don't let it get away. Find a way.

5.

First Car, Second Love

After Dad and I walked away from the '57 Pontiac, we set out to track down the other "looker" of the evening, the '59 Chevy Impala. To this day I don't know what ever possessed me to even consider buying the same make and model of car as my friend Jerry's. It might have been because he was always bragging about how whatever he had was the absolute best—I guess I just wanted a chance to show him up for once. Between that and having 300 bucks burning a hole in my pocket, I felt an urgent need to get my own set of wheels and quit driving around in Mom's '61 Ford Galaxy.

KEYLESS IN SEATTLE

The second address was pretty easy to find and I spotted the Chevy from a block away. It looked great from a distance and even better as we drove up the driveway. Aside from a couple of cracked windows, this blue and white looker seemed to be in decent shape. The owners seemed nice, though a little evasive. In my quest to buy my first set of wheels I was about to make a couple of big mistakes. For starters there was no key for the trunk (the owners said it was lost). "No problem," I thought. "I can just have one made." The Chevy drove fine and sported a big 348-cubic-inch V8, which I was sure had a lot more muscle than Jerry's 283. I smiled at the thought of leaving Jerry in the dust, as if we would one day be squaring off at the racetrack. I convinced myself it had to be worth every bit of the $200 asking price. "Don't want to let this cherry of a car get away," I thought to myself as I made a full-price offer. Such a deal. There was no key to the trunk, but it did have plates on it. "Sold!" said the friendly man in the checkered pants.

Dad had been pretty quiet up to this point, then he piped up with what I thought was a totally off-the-wall question.

"Does this car have a clear title?" he asked pointedly, seeming to suspect something amiss.

My first thought was, "What's a title?"

"Yes it does!" the nice man replied. "I can get that for you tomorrow."

"Sounds good," I said, shaking his hand. "I'll take it!"

We agreed to return the following evening to pick up the Chevy with the title. I tossed and turned all night, dreaming of owning my very own car. My dream was about to come true and I could hardly wait.

We returned the next night for the car and title, and it was so good to have my own set of wheels! I felt such independence and so grown up. One Sunday afternoon a couple of months later, as I was driving to the local high school to play basketball with some friends, I heard a banging sound coming from the front end. I pulled over and discovered that the banging stopped as soon as the car did. That should have been a big clue, but I missed it. I popped open the hood and peered around but didn't see anything that looked out of place. Then I walked around the car, still puzzled about the source of the banging. With the mystery unsolved, I got back in the car and resumed my drive to the school, but as soon as the car was rolling, the banging started up again.

Later that night a couple of friends came over to look under the hood to see if they could see anything, but there again, no luck. The banging started up whenever the car started moving. For the next few days I drove the back roads and stayed away from other drivers. Whenever I accelerated, the banging sped up too, and to make matters worse, it was getting progressively louder.

THE BIG CRASH

The very next day it happened. I was taking the back road home when the noise suddenly got really loud and the whole front of the car began to shudder uncontrollably. And then disaster struck. Before I could even hit the brakes, there was a loud crash as the left front tire came off and the whole left front corner of the Chevy slammed down on the axle. The Chevy pulled wildly to the right, and it was all I could do to stop the beast.

Knees shaking, I climbed out of the car to survey the damage and collect my wits. The runaway tire was nowhere in sight, and it took a while to find that it had rolled off the road, down an embankment, and into a creek. It was no easy task to fetch the tire out of the creek and wrestle it all the way up the steep bank. By the time I made it back up to the road, I was huffing and puffing like a race horse. I jacked up the car and managed to get the wheel back on, using a lug nut from each of the other three wheels to cinch the runaway tire back in its rightful place. When I resumed my trip home, the mysterious banging had ceased once and for all. And though I was glad the runaway tire or crippled Chevy hadn't hit anybody, I found myself even more relieved that nobody had witnessed this embarrassing scene. I chose to keep this episode to myself.

THE BIGGER CRASH

The Chevy turned out to be a pretty decent car (aside from wiring problems) and served me well for almost a year. Some baby moon hubcaps dressed it up, and I loved driving it to school during my junior year of high school. Its life was abruptly cut short one night while I was driving home from my Aunt Margaret's place. I was traveling down a gravel road that was cut into a hillside, leaving the hill on one side and a steep embankment on the other with no guardrail. (This just happened to be the very same road on which I had lost my tire!) I rounded a curve at about 25 miles per hour and was met head-on by a VW Squareback station wagon traveling on *my* side of the road. I wrenched the wheel to the right but not fast enough to avoid a collision. The Chevy started to slide and hit the VW head on, spinning it completely around. Miraculously, no one was seriously injured, but the VW was totaled and my Chevy was towed home with a badly crumpled left front fender smashed over the left front tire.

What I liked: This baby was definitely faster than Jerry's Impala.

What I learned: Don't forget to tighten the lug nuts, and, yes, you will need a key for the trunk.

6.

Seconds, Anyone?

By the time my '59 Chevy Impala had suffered its crushing injury, Jerry had moved on to his second car, a white '62 Dodge convertible. His '59 Impala had made its way back to the family that had sold it to him in the first place—I never quite figured out why.

In need of a new left fender and grill, I decided to approach them to see if they would consider selling the Chevy for the second time. They obliged and 80 bucks later it was mine. My plan was to remove the fender and grill and scrap the rest, but after comparing the two Impalas (not to mention Dad's ultimatum that one of them had to go), I decided to buy Jerry's old one and fix it up.

Remember the old Dragnet TV series—the one that began each episode with "What you are about to hear is the truth, the whole truth, and nothing but the truth"? The same applies here: as farfetched as it might seem, what you are about to read is the truth, the whole truth, and nothing but the truth.

Right after I took possession of Jerry's old car, I decided that the faded yellow paint job needed some luster. I had admired a sporty new yellow Camaro with a black vinyl top that had two black rectangles painted on the hood and came up with a plan to give my old Chevy a similar treatment. After carefully masking out two rectangles on the hood, I painted them flat black—more precisely, I *brushed* them on. Pleased with the improvement, I instantly visualized transforming this ole Chevy into my very own muscle car. (As if somebody might mistake this '59 Chevy for a '69 Camaro.) With my $2 paintbrush, I carefully brushed flat black paint over the entire roof, imagining I was duplicating the looks of a vinyl roof.

Driving around town during the next couple of days, I couldn't help but notice that my sporty black roof and rectangles were raising a few eyebrows and generating quite a stir among my friends. Jerry didn't say much, so I logically concluded he was jealous of my artistic flair. Their comments propelled me to take this custom paint scheme to another level. I remember thinking that if this baby looked this good with the flat black roof and rectangles, just think how sweet she'll look if that faded yellow was bright yellow, just like that cool Camaro. My next move? I marched straight down to the auto parts store and bought some bright yellow paint. In the privacy of my parents' garage, I proceeded to paint every square inch of the old Chevy . . . with a brush.

I was eager to drive my show stopper into the church parking lot the next Sunday. In retrospect, it was probably good that I had the windows rolled up and couldn't hear all the comments my paint job received. No, I was sure that I had all the makings of one hot machine. I wish I could say that my creative juices quit flowing right there—but I was on a roll.

BAD TO WORSE

Next, I focused my attention on the interior. Thanks to my part-time job at a carpet store, I had access to dozens of carpet samples, a variety of which I installed on the car floor and inside up on the roof. But I wasn't satisfied yet. Determined to turn my aged Chevy into a Camaro look-a-like, there came the desire for bucket seats. I built my own console out of plywood and cut a chunk out of the front bench seat so that I could install it. In the process I realized that full-length front seats have a steel plate at the top to make them rigid. Duh! Cutting through that steel plate made for some very saggy seats. What an idiot, right? I shudder to think what Dad might have said had he strolled up and saw me cutting through the front seat with a hack saw! I've come to realize that my dad was a very patient man.

By now you may be wondering why this moron didn't buy that '57 Pontiac in the first place. I've often wondered this myself. I've even wondered why my dad didn't advise me to buy the Pontiac, or why neither one of my parents commented on the insane "improvements" I made to the Chevy. I'm sure they made plenty of comments to each other as they were counting the days until I finished high school and joined the military, or better yet, the circus.

MAROONED

After a few months of driving around in my bright yellow muscle car, I began thinking that this wild paint job on my old '59 Chevy seemed a bit too bold—maybe it was time to tone it down a little. The answer? Another trip to the auto parts store for more paint, this time a dark reddish maroon. I even talked my best friend, Steve, into helping me paint the Chevy—this time we each had a brush. I finished the job by using flat black paint on the chrome strips that ran along the full length of the body on both sides. At the time I thought of this sophisticated combination as a one-of-a-kind classic, but of course most folks would have described it as downright butt ugly.

Soon after, I graduated from high school, enlisted in the Navy, and needed to peddle the Chevy before heading for boot camp. After all, leaving it parked in Dad's driveway wasn't an option. Having had no luck from the advertisement that I ran in the local classifieds (I wonder why?), I kept lowering my sights and finally succumbed to calling various wrecking yards in search of a buyer. After several declines, one wrecking yard manager responded with, "Sure! We'll give you anywhere from 15 to 300 bucks for your car! Bring it on over with your title." Bingo!

I was so excited about all the things I could do with $300 that I could hardly contain myself. The Chevy must have sensed its own demise as I approached the wrecking yard because it backfired when I parked and let off a big puff of blue smoke from the tail end with white smoke billowing from under the dash. Nonetheless, I jumped out to greet the man who would soon be forking over a roll of crisp fifty dollar bills for the opportunity to add this classic car to his collection.

But as the saying goes, "Things are not always what they appear on the surface." The wrecking-yard manager came sauntering out of the building with his clipboard and slowly walked around the Chevy, muttering something under his breath that I mistakenly interpreted as utter glee for the chance to nab this classy chassis for a measly 300 bucks.

He cleared his throat and spit in the dirt, then rubbed his stubbly chin. "Well, s—t," he spoke slowly. "I'll give you fifteen dollars for her." I couldn't believe what I was hearing.

"Fifteen dollars?" I asked. "But you said anywhere from $15 to $300!"

He looked at me and spit again. Then he let me have it with both barrels.

"Son, there ain't a damn thing on this crate to salvage. Fifteen bucks. Take it or leave it." I took it and never looked back.

What I liked: It was nice to have my own set of wheels.

What I learned: Never paint a car with a brush. Never!

7.
The Grand Safari

It was August 1970, Richard Nixon was in the White House, and the Vietnam War was in full swing. I enlisted in the U.S. Navy's two-by-six program, which meant that I would serve for two years on active duty and be on reserve status for four years. With boot camp behind me I was a free man until June 1971, the scheduled time for me to leave for active duty.

During the ten months between boot camp and active duty, I worked as a busboy at a new restaurant named John Henry's, a snazzy little place (for our town anyway) with a railroad motif. And I was dating Annie, a girl from my town who attended a private college in Seattle and lived in the dormitory.

Since I was making so many roundtrips from my suburban home in Alderwood Manor to Seattle to see Annie, it was time to buy some new wheels. I was still haunted by the memory of the junkyard dawg forking over fifteen lousy bucks for my customized Chevy Impala. I had learned a lot, however, in a few short months and had decided that brush painting should be left for the artist to express on canvas, not on an innocent car.

Yes, this young sailor was determined to make a move up to something more sophisticated than an old clunker Chevy. While my high school buddies were salivating over the must-have '57 Chevys, I knew that they were far beyond my reach. Besides, I was marching to the beat of a different drummer (*way* different, as evidenced by the car-painting fiasco).

I had always liked the styling of the 1959-1960 Pontiacs, so I decided to start there. While scanning the classifieds, I found an ad for a 1960 Pontiac Grand Safari station wagon. I called the Pontiac dealer, who insisted, "This cream puff won't last long at $149!" So I borrowed Mom's Ford and drove up for a look. There in the back row sat this gorgeous turquoise and white wagon that seemed to have my name written all over it. It reminded me of the 1959 models, which gave me all the more reason to want it.

The Pontiac came with a big 389-cubic-inch engine and a four-barrel carburetor. This car would go like a bat out of you-know-where, and I was instantly hooked after my first drive. Now older and wiser, I asked Dad to check it out, too. I was sure that his only regret would be that he couldn't have it for himself. I mean after all, he was still driving around town in that old '57 Ford pickup.

Dad agreed to go along for a test drive that evening and while doing so—being the sensible, down to earth man that he was— he asked me to try the brakes. I guess we were traveling about 45 miles per hour on dry asphalt when I stomped on the brake pedal. That's when all four tires locked up and the Pontiac came to a screeching halt amid a cloud of blue smoke from the burning rubber. The guy in the car behind me must have wet his pants as he swerved to avoid a nasty rear ender. This was my first experience with power brakes, and the jolt nearly propelled Dad (who wasn't wearing a seatbelt—it wasn't the law in those days) straight through the windshield. Dad was a deeply religious man and I don't recall ever hearing him swear as I was growing up. He must have come drastically close to it that day, though, as he made reference to a couple of names that must be buried somewhere deep in the Old Testament of the Bible. The rest of the test drive was pretty calm and we drove along in silence. I couldn't help but wonder what Dad was thinking, but decided not to rock the boat as we returned to the dealership. We were greeted by the salesman, who was ready to write up a sales order. "Nice car," I said smiling as I handed him the keys. Trying to sound mature and confident, I continued, "I want to think it over and will let you know."

The next morning Dad phoned from work and suggested that I keep looking and consider spending a little more to get a better car, maybe something in the $500 to $600 range. Thinking back over what I had put him through with the Chevys, not to mention the test drive the night before in the Pontiac, I was just glad he was still willing to talk to me.

He must have been counting the days until I headed for active duty with the Navy. Although I had my heart set on the Pontiac, I had to agree that his suggestion made sense. And after all, I did have about eight hundred bucks in the bank. I fed him a line about not wanting to spend my vast savings on a car because I wanted to take care of my other expenses (which basically amounted to insurance and fun money).

"Okay," he sighed. "It's your money."

I was thrilled at these words and took them as another green light to proceed. Two days later the turquoise and white Pontiac was parked in our driveway.

ANNIE'S PANTIES

The Pontiac ran pretty well and was a real cruiser. I promptly installed an A-OO-GA horn, which made for some good fun. Annie liked it, too. I would pick her up from college most Friday nights to bring her home for the weekend. One night as we drove home for the weekend, Annie nestled close, telling me all about her busy week at school. At one point I had to jab on the brakes, which sent her small duffle bag flipping upside down, spilling its contents onto the floor of the front seat.

"Sorry 'bout that, sweetheart," I said as she leaned forward to gather up the contents and put them back into the bag.

"No problem, honey," she purred lovingly with a smile as she patted my leg.

Saturday came and went way too fast. On Sunday morning I was on my way out the door for church when Dad asked me for a ride.

"Sure," I answered proudly, glad that he was willing to take another ride in the Pontiac. "I'll go warm up the engine."

I was warming up the car when Dad came out of the house and headed in my direction. He had almost reached the car when something on the floor caught my eye. Glancing down I discovered a pair of Annie's pink panties, which must have spilled out of her duffle bag. In the nick of time I tossed them under the seat, shuddering to think of the lecture that would have gone well past the end of the second church service had Dad seen the panties on the floor. Whew . . .

GENTLEMEN, START YOUR ENGINES

Before my departure for active duty, I was required to attend monthly weekend Navy Reserve drills. I dreaded these drills because it meant I couldn't see Annie until late Sunday. One long, cold weekend drill in January seemed to last forever, and I couldn't wait to see my sweetheart for at least a couple of hours before she headed back to the college dormitory.

The speedometer on the Pontiac had just passed 80 miles per hour as I roared down the freeway, anxious for a kiss and warm embrace from my sweet Annie. The engine sputtered a bit as the needle passed 85 miles per hour, and I drove the gas pedal to the floor. The engine suddenly faltered, and as I glanced at the rearview mirror, blue smoke rolled out of the Pontiac's tail end. This was definitely not a good sign, especially not now. I let up on the gas and kept going, but by the time I reached home the engine was running pretty rough.

With the help of two mechanically inclined friends, I surveyed the damage and discovered that the Pontiac had blown a piston. This was annoying at first but proved to be a good learning experience as the three of us took the engine apart, replaced the piston and rings, and had it back in service within a week. A test drive proved that thanks to our collective skill and mechanical expertise, everything was back to normal. Except for one thing: there was still a coffee can half full of nuts and bolts that had come from somewhere in the depths of that giant engine; they had somehow failed to find their way back. I decided to keep them handy just in case.

SUNDAY DRIVE

Over time the Pontiac developed a pinhole leak somewhere in the brake line. Routine stops were never a problem, but a quick panic stop would squeeze the brake fluid out of the line and onto the pavement. My low-dollar remedy for this problem was to simply stop the car and add more fluid to the master cylinder. "After all," I had assured myself, "I can buy a whole lot of brake fluid for the price of an entire brake job!"

One gorgeous spring afternoon, Annie and I decided to take a Sunday drive. She was once again nestled close to my side on the wide bench seat as we drove along the winding country road. A dog ran out in front of us, forcing me to swerve and slam on the brakes to avoid sending the pooch into orbit. Continuing on I reminded myself that I would need to add more brake fluid. I certainly didn't want to alarm my sweet little Annie.

The ride continued for a time until we started down a very long hill that I certainly hadn't planned to include in my itinerary. The brake pedal went all the way to the floor when I pushed it, and I knew we were in for a wild ride. Trying to appear calm, I stifled a scream as the Pontiac picked up speed.

"Aren't you going a little fast?" Annie asked innocently as she snuggled a little closer.

"We're fine," I replied trying to sound confident as I stared in horror at what was ahead. There in the middle of this very long hill were railroad tracks crossing the road. One didn't need to be a mathematician to unravel the problem that was looming at breakneck speed. I don't remember the angle of the hill other than "steep," but I do remember that the railroad track was level. The old Pontiac was doing at least 50 miles per hour when we hit the tracks: I was certain that both front tires and shocks were going to blow right through the fenders.

All I heard was KA-BOOM when the Pontiac careened over the tracks and continued barreling down the hill.

In a matter of seconds I realized that we had just jumped out of the frying pan and into the fire, for less than a quarter mile ahead the road took a sharp curve to the right. The railroad tracks had mercifully slowed our descent, but it took all the strength I could muster (and a host of guardian angels, no doubt) to keep that Pontiac from flying off the road and into a cow pasture as we rounded the curve. As the car slowed to a stop, I looked over at Annie, who was white as a sheet.

"Are you okay?" I stammered.

Annie nodded slightly and I'm sure she was thinking that I was trying to kill both of us.

"What are you trying to do?" she finally hissed through clenched teeth. I had never seen Annie this steamed.

"Ah, I guess I need to check those brakes," I confessed, trying to reassure her as I got out and refilled the now-empty master cylinder with more brake fluid.

FREEWAY FRENZY

When my next weekend Navy drill rolled around, we were scheduled for a Friday-night ship inspection from the base's commanding officer. I put on my woolen dress blues and met my folks for dinner before heading to the ship.

My folks smiled as I entered the restaurant.

"You look so nice in your uniform, son," Mom said proudly, probably hoping that the other patrons would take notice.

"Thanks, Mom," I replied as I sat down at their table.

The proud bubble burst as Dad got right to the point.

"Do you have a spare tire in that car yet?" He asked intently, as if he had been waiting all day to ask me.

"Ah, yeah, I do," I lied, knowing full well that I had never bothered to even look.

"That's good," he continued. "You never know when you'll need one."

"Right, Dad," I replied, wondering why he kept nagging me about the spare tire.

We enjoyed a good dinner together, and after bidding them farewell I headed for the ship.

The old Pontiac was again cruising at about 70 miles per hour, and I was thinking about Annie, our future, and anything *but* the upcoming inspection. I couldn't wait to see her on Sunday.

A familiar KA-BOOM jarred me to reality; this time it was the right front tire blowing out and scaring me big time. After shooting across three lanes of traffic, I wrestled the car onto the shoulder and tried to regain my composure.

"I guess it's time to check on that spare tire," I muttered to myself as I got out and moved to the rear end of the Pontiac to open the tailgate. Guess what? No spare tire and no jack. With the inspection in less than two hours, there was no time to spare (okay, bad pun) so I hopped into the Pontiac and limped down the shoulder for half a mile to the next freeway exit. There wasn't much tire left by the time I made it to the nearest gas station nearly a mile up the road. The attendant must have felt sorry for me as I unraveled my predicament. He went around the back of the station and returned a few minutes later with an old tire he had pulled out of the dumpster. I thanked him profusely as he mounted it and offered him all the money I had in my wallet, the entire $2. The tire was a couple sizes too small and had a plug in it, but it did the job, and I passed inspection on the ship. A couple months later I did get some new tires and a jack—but I could never bear to tell Dad the story.

The Pontiac was still running strong when I was ready to leave for active duty. I sold it to some family friends for a whopping $200; I think the A-OO-GA horn was a major selling point.

What I liked: Gasoline was 29 cents a gallon in 1971.

What I learned: Take time to check out that spare tire. Dad really does know best.

8.

Wild Pony

Before joining the Navy, I considered myself a pretty well-adjusted guy who knew a little about a lot of things. But my experience in boot camp and commissary training school showed me that there was a whole side of life that I had never seen before. In June 1971 it was time for me to report for my two years of active duty. My first duty station was with VA-215, an attack squadron (nicknamed the Barn Owls) based at Naval Air Station (NAS) Lemoore, California. I met up with the squadron in the Philippines, where they were finishing a deployment aboard the USS *Oriskany*, one of the older aircraft carriers in the fleet.

BACK ON DRY LAND

When the deployment ended in December in Alameda, California, the squadron personnel boarded buses and headed back to NAS Lemoore, a place I had only heard about. On the buses, airmen talked excitedly about how good it was to be "back home." But as the new guy, all I knew was that I was headed for unknown territory somewhere in California. Even so, I was secretly thankful to be off the ship and on dry land for a few months.

We arrived at Lemoore in the middle of the night. The next morning, the sun rose high into the December sky, but I was still feeling very much in the dark about this strange new place. I would soon learn that Lemoore is nestled in the San Joaquin Valley in central California, thirty-some miles from Fresno. As a commissary man, I was assigned to the mess hall on the base, where my job was to issue food to the cooks and bakers for their use in preparing meals for base personnel.

Though the Navy provided bus service on base, I found myself longing to have my own set of wheels. What better way to explore my new surroundings in central California! My commanding officer was selling his 1966 Ford Mustang, complete with 289 cubic inches of engine and a sporty stick shift. Nine hundred dollars later I had the keys in hand to this silver-blue coupe, feeling very much on top of the world. After all, this was a huge step up from the Pontiac: I definitely felt that I had arrived.

FOGGED IN

One winter evening as I headed into the town of Lemoore to visit friends, I discovered a heavy blanket of fog had settled in, making visibility beyond a few feet virtually impossible. The interstate had two lanes in each direction separated by a wide grassy median. Even as I crept through the dense fog I still managed to miss the exit into town. Not wanting to be late (or to get lost) I slowed to a crawl and pulled an illegal U-turn across not one but two sets of double yellow lines in the median.

"There you go," I told myself smugly, feeling as if I had just gotten away with a major no-no. I was groovin' now. Reality snapped me back to attention as I again drove past the exit into town.

"No prob-o-lemo," I muttered to myself, cranking the wheel to the left and again crossing the double yellow line in the thick fog. As the Mustang's headlights swept across the median to complete my second illegal U-turn within five minutes, a silhouette appeared on the far outside shoulder of the lanes I was entering. There in the fog sat a California State Patrol car, complete with lights and siren that lit up like a Christmas tree before I had even completed my U-turn. Little did I know that I was about to meet the biggest state trooper I had ever laid eyes on. When he walked up to the Mustang, I was eye level with his belt buckle.

This was destined to be a night of "firsts": First drive in dense fog, first illegal U-turn, first encounter with the police, first major ass-chewing (outside of boot camp), and, oh yes, first ticket. Despite the grilling, I kept my wits about me and decided not to disclose the fact that I had just completed not one but two illegal U-turns in less than five minutes. After all, I knew I couldn't afford to lose much more of my backside, not to mention wind up with a heftier ticket.

I had the option to "pay up" as charged or go through the mitigation process to explain the circumstances to a judge. Opting for the latter, I was sure that any judge in the county would understand my plight and let me off the hook. After all, here was a clean-cut young sailor who took a little break from the line of duty and happened to make an illegal U-turn in the fog. No big deal—it was a mistake anyone could make. Right? Wrong. No slack was given to this poor soul: I had to pay up, all nineteen bucks. I decided it was in my best interest to obey the law, especially in Lemoore, California.

TEN LONG MONTHS

Several months later it was time to ship out again, this time on board the USS *Enterprise*, the Navy's first nuclear-powered aircraft carrier. The *Enterprise* was based in Alameda, California, and I decided to park the Mustang on base in a storage lot designated for long-term parking. I covered the car with a sheet of heavy plastic and headed out to sea for what was to be one of the longest cruises ever in the Western Pacific.

Some ten months later, the Vietnam War was over, and so was my time on active duty with the Navy. The *Enterprise* sailed under the Golden Gate Bridge to an exciting homecoming welcome. The San Francisco fireboats escorted us with water shooting high into the morning sky. The Golden Gate Bridge was lined with well wishers proudly waving American flags. The pier was jammed with hundreds of cheering families who were anxiously awaiting a long-overdue reunion and warm embrace from their sailors, their husbands, their sons, their brothers, their dads.

I could hardly wait for my own reunion with Annie, but I still had one week of active duty remaining, which gave me time to retrieve the Mustang from storage and get it ready for the drive home to Washington State.

As I entered the storage lot, I was excited to free my wild pony from this corral of tired old cars. To my dismay I found that two of the tires were flat, and that the plastic covering had melted into the roof, hood, and trunk lid. But it was still like a reunion with an old friend, and within an hour the Mustang was towed to the garage on base for a tune-up, an oil change, and four new tires. I'd decide later what to do about the melted plastic in the paint—one thing was for sure, it wouldn't involve a paint brush.

ONE HOT PONY

Sure enough, one week later I was a free man, headed for home in my silver-blue pony laden with treasures from various ports of call. The miles were flying by as I headed up Interstate 5 into Northern California. It was early afternoon when the Mustang started to shudder and the temperature gauge went well past the H for hot. Fortunately, I was right by a rest stop, so I turned off the engine and coasted down the hill into the parking lot. This was somewhere south of Redding and it was hot, hot, and hot. I noticed that every vehicle in the parking lot had one thing in common: the hoods were all open like parched mouths in the desert thirsty for a cool drink.

Checking under the hood didn't tell me much other than this was one hot pony car. Being somewhat challenged in the mechanical department (remember the engine rebuild on the Pontiac?), I poked around, unsure of what to look for. Trying not to touch what I knew would be hot (which didn't leave much), I spotted water seeping out of the engine side of the radiator. Looking closer, I saw arch-shaped nicks in the radiator. I then noted that the fan was loose as well, not a pretty picture for sure. The hoses seemed to be in good shape, but I knew that the Mustang needed more than a drink (and so did I) before this afternoon was over.

It was time to call for help. The phone at this particular rest stop was out of service, much like all the overheated cars and drivers sitting around baking in the scorching sunshine. Remember this was 1973, and the only "cell" phones in those days were located at the city jail.

After asking around, I learned that the nearest town was less than five miles up the interstate. "I can make that," I assured myself. "I *have* to make that."

The only container I had to carry water in was a plastic tub from the trunk that held a few tools and cleaning supplies. After several trips to the water faucet, I was able to cool the engine down. After filling the radiator, I refilled the tub, hoping that it would be enough to make it to the next town for needed repairs.

Only one problem remained. Where do I put the tub of water? This pony car was packed to the roof with precious cargo. I saw only one solution: I set it on the floor in front of me.

You can be sure that driving the next few miles was challenging. Science was never my favorite class, but I seemed to recall something about the laws of physics/displacement, which were about to be demonstrated over the next five miles. The water in the tub sensed every car movement and responded accordingly, sloshing back and forth, threatening to spill over the sides and flood the floor. Shifting gears only added to the challenge, as I navigated my crippled pony car to the nearest garage for repairs.

After stopping twice to add more water, I nursed the Mustang up the road to the little town of Cottonwood, turned off the engine, and rolled into the one-and-only car repair shop. Two seasoned mechanics, looking somewhat bored, sauntered over. The wall thermometer read 102 degrees, and a big ceiling fan kept the hot air moving as they peered under the hood to diagnose the stricken pony. A big old dog lay stretched out on the concrete floor, uninterested in any visitors.

It didn't take them long to find the problem. The bearings in the water pump had failed, loosening up the fan that grazed the radiator, resulting in the arched shaped nicks. My lucky day indeedy. With renewed vigor, the two mechanics removed the radiator and water pump within minutes. Leaving me and the dog to mind the garage, these old pros took off in two different directions, one to get the radiator fixed and the other to round up a new water pump. In a way I felt like they had me over a barrel and could take me all the way to the cleaners and back. On the other hand, they had trusted me enough to leave me alone in their shop, so somehow I knew I could, in turn, trust these two veteran mechanics.

They both returned less than an hour later and resumed work on the Mustang, but by this time all I could think about was getting an ice-cold drink. I decided that once the car was fixed, I was going to get me a cold six pack and stop at the first motel with a pool.

The two mechanics had my pony back in service within an hour. They had done all the work, but I was the one sweating like a moose. I wasn't sure if it was due to enduring the wait in the 102-degree garage or anticipating the repair bill they were going to hand me.

Fifty-nine dollars later I was on my way out of Cottonwood and back on Interstate 5 in search of that motel with a pool. I found one in Redding, checked in, and headed straight for the pool. My first day as a civilian had been a dilly, but I was a free man and life was good! I gazed fondly at my pony car and knew that both of us would be ready to ride in the morning. There were many miles that stretched out ahead of us, and I looked forward to riding them out together. My Annie was only two days away and I couldn't wait to kiss her warm, soft lips, hold her tight, and never let her go.

I hit the sack early that night and slept like a baby as my pony waited patiently for sunrise and the chance to carry me back to Annie, the other love of my life. I couldn't wait to get home.

What I liked: My first car with a stick shift.

What I learned: Next time try a car cover instead of plastic.

9.

Vista Cruisin'

It has been said that hindsight is 20/20. Here I was, fresh out of the Navy with a tidy stash of cash, and I was ready to go car shopping again. This was fueled by my sweetie's first drive behind the wheel of the Mustang. When she let out the clutch, the pony bucked and squealed all over the street. My otherwise-calm demeanor went right out the window along with a few choice words that I had picked up in the Navy overseas.

Less than five minutes into Annie's inaugural drive of the Mustang, I was convinced that she was either going to kill the pony or our relationship. She pulled up to a stop sign, and wouldn't you know it some poor soul in a Buick pulled up right behind her. Our little ride was rapidly turning into a drive from hell.

"Give it some gas and let the clutch out easy," I hissed

through clenched teeth.

"Stop shouting at me!" she shot back as she gunned the engine and took her foot off the clutch. After laying down a four-foot patch of rubber, the bucking pony and I were both done.

"Get out of the damn car!" I hollered angrily as I burst out of the car and slammed the door. Annie quickly complied, scurrying around the car and into the passenger seat. I got behind the wheel, fired up all 289 cubic inches under the Pony's hood, then added another four feet of rubber on the pavement as the guy in the Buick sat there with his mouth hanging open.

By the following Saturday I was cruising the local car lots to see what kind of hot rod would catch my fancy. And then I saw it, right there at the local Ford dealership. I spotted the car that I would have given my left arm for just four years earlier: a beautiful green 1969 Olds Vista Cruiser wagon with the authentic fake wood trim. My, oh my! It was as if time had stopped. My heart raced as I walked around it and then slid in behind the wheel. I just had to have it, white walls and all.

I determined later that the salesman had seen me coming and scored big time with the sale of the century. I mean, really! How many other days had he (or anyone for that matter) seen some kid drive up in a Mustang with a pocket full of cash and trade it in on an Oldsmobile station wagon? He's probably still babbling about it at some old folks home in Nebraska.

As for me, I was in seventh heaven with my new wheels. The Olds served us well through key milestones, including our honeymoon, numerous camping trips, and the births of our first two children, Kevin and Mark. There are so many great memories! The Vista Cruiser had a moon roof, which made for great stargazing while cuddling with my sweetie with the rear seats folded down. Annie would later remark that one of our children may have been conceived during one of those stargazing sessions. What a car!

HORN A PLENTY

It was a very hot July afternoon as Annie, Kevin, Mark, and I rolled into the local drive-in for some lunch and cold drinks. The place was jam packed and the car hops were really hustling to take care of all the customers. My sweaty little family and I rolled down all the windows and sat there with the headlights on, waiting to order.

After we ordered, I happened to be running a quarter that I was holding around the big padded center section of the steering wheel. And then the unthinkable happened. The quarter disappeared inside the steering wheel and the horn starting blowing. (No, I am not making this up.)

You can just imagine the mayhem that erupted. The poor car hop, who just happened to be scurrying by the Olds at the "point of contact," nearly lost her heaping tray full of burgers and fries. Most people stared, undoubtedly annoyed, while others started hollering as I frantically tried to pull the steering wheel apart with my bare hands. No such luck.

With the horn still blowing, I jumped out of the car and lifted the hood in search of a wire to pull. Make a note here: a car horn actually grows several decibels louder when the hood is open. I've never cared for loud noises, not to mention drawing this kind of attention to myself. I reached down and grabbed the horn wires and yanked them loose, skinning the knuckles on my right hand in the process. The blaring horn stopped just in time for everyone within a three-block radius to hear me let loose a ration of Navy jargon, and I'm not talking about the words to "Anchors Aweigh." I shut the hood and got back in the car, avoiding eye contact with the gawking onlookers.

Our food hadn't arrived yet, and I could just imagine what the cook and one particular car hop might be doing to our burgers back there in the kitchen. I felt trapped. I considered just leaving without the food, but I would still have a hungry family, and I fully expected that the restaurant people might send the police after me. But if I stayed, would I really want to eat the food? I shuddered as I had a flashback and remembered what my friend Dickie and I had done to another kid's popcorn at the movies.

Fortunately for all of us, Annie thought the whole scene was pretty comical. When our food finally came and the car hop actually smiled at me, I relaxed a little. It must have been a hoot to serve up some hamburgers and fries to a first-class jack ass. I wondered too if this innocent girl had ever heard my particular line of Navy jargon. I thanked her profusely for the food, drinks, and even the napkins and straws.

People in the surrounding cars finally stopped staring and resumed their festive drive-in experience. We had no doubt given them something to talk about, and I never will be sure what was on my hamburger, but I ate every bite. Even with the horn disconnected, I was paranoid about touching the steering wheel for fear of setting off another round of chaos. I laid down the biggest tip I'd ever left, and my two young boys had picked up some new words that I would have to explain later.

RAINDROPS KEEP FALLIN' AND FALLIN'

The Pacific Northwest is known for the rain, and as the years rolled by the Olds started to rust around the windows in the top. This made for damp carpets and a smelly interior, no matter how much window sealer or how many car fresheners we tried. I knew it was time to take action when I found mushrooms growing under the rear seat. With a mortgage payment and two little boys by now, my pockets weren't stuffed full of cash like they had been in my single days.

Upon surveying the rust in the roof, I enlisted the help and advice of a guy I'll call Mr. Hardbody, who did auto body and paint work out of his home. He saw a golden opportunity when I showed up with the Olds and convinced me that the car would look great once he got rid of the rust and painted the whole car. The price seemed right and he said he could start right away. Annie and I studied Hardbody's color chart and chose what we thought would be an attractive color (similar to avocado green). We were excited to think that within just a week the Vista Cruiser would look brand new. After a couple of delays, Hardbody called with the welcome news that our chariot was ready for viewing.

We raced out to the Hardbody's home, talking about how nice it would be to have the Olds looking just like new. Actually, I did all the talking and Annie just smiled and looked out the window. What was she thinking? Her silence should have been another clue, but I didn't pick up on it at the time.

Upon arrival at the Hardbody's home, I was ready to hear a drum roll as Mr. Hardbody opened the garage door. As he lifted the garage door, I gasped at the sight of the Olds: The paint was alarmingly brighter than I remembered from the little color swatch in the brochure. In fact, I'd seen some taxicabs this color, but never an Olds Vista Cruiser. Hardbody was prepared: Without saying a word, he pulled from his pocket the color sample that we had selected and held it up to the car. Yikes! A perfect match.

The color never really did tone down much, it just kind of grew on us. Over the course of the following months, I learned that rust is difficult if not impossible to stop. It can be cut out or slowed down, but for the Olds the old rust started showing through the new paint job within a few months. When the day came to finally sell it, the Olds had served us well for over seven years—moon roof, mushrooms, and all.

What I liked: Stargazing with Annie.

What I learned: Never base a color selection on a sample the size of a postage stamp.

10.

Dodge in the Garage

In the early years of our marriage, what with going to school and working, we found ourselves needing a second car. After reviewing our finances, we wanted to be sensible and decided to find something within our budget. I wasn't sure what we would find with a whopping $500: we would soon learn that it wouldn't buy you much of a car, not even in 1975.

I answered a newspaper ad and found a yellow 1966 Dodge Coronet sitting in the owner's garage with an asking price of $450. The body was straight and the interior was clean. What's more, the owner seemed pretty honest. After a drive around the block I decided it would do the job—and when I offered $400 cash, the owner gladly accepted. It was certainly no sports car, but it promised some good, reliable transportation at a fair price.

On the drive home I decided to see what kind of zip the

Dodge had under the hood. Before I even had a chance to punch the pedal, I started hearing a howling noise coming from the rear end when the speedometer hit anything above 35 miles per hour. Now I knew why the previous owner had so readily accepted my 400 bucks.

SOMETHING FISHY

Annie's dad *loved* to fish. Her parents had a twenty-two-foot boat moored at the nearby Edmonds boat harbor, which is where we could find her dad most weekends. He knew all the places for fishing and used all the right gear to catch some of the best-tasting salmon I've ever eaten. Next to Annie, his boat was his pride and joy and he loved being on the water.

It was early Saturday morning after a dark, stormy night in November when Annie and I were awakened by a phone call from her mom.

"Dad's boat sank last night," she sighed heavily. "The waves were heavy and came over the transom, which lowered the back of the boat. More water came in as it got lower and then it finally went under. The only thing sticking up is the bow, which is still tied up at the dock. Dad got a call from the harbormaster this morning. Can you come and help us?" she asked anxiously.

Her words hit hard; we were stunned. Dad had owned the boat for years and it was practically part of the family. "We'll be right there," Annie blurted, trying to comfort her mom.

We jumped into the Dodge for the short drive to the boat harbor. From our vantage point on the dock we saw her, lying mostly submerged in the now-calm waters. Her bow stuck out of the water as if she was gasping for air and hanging on for dear life. The bow line was her lifeline as it was still tied to the dock, keeping her from going under altogether.

More family members joined us on the dock to mourn the tragedy. The mood was somber as I looked from face to face. Annie's dad looked as if he was ready to cry.

Divers had already arrived with the harbormaster and had put a strap under the aft end of the boat so that it could be winched up out of the water. Pumps removed the water from the boat as the winches raised it. Although the process was long and tedious, we stood by to watch the old boat gradually rise from its watery grave.

Once enough water had been pumped out, the boat floated on its own. The harbor personnel towed it to the place where it could be hoisted out of the water and onto the boat trailer. Annie's dad had gone for the trailer, which hadn't been used in years.

The family looked on anxiously as the scene unfolded, wondering if Dad's boat would ever be seaworthy again.

With the trailer in place, the boat was slowly lowered into position where it could finally rest out of the water. More bad news: one of the trailer tires was flat. The boat was once again lifted up so that we could jack up the trailer and change the tire. The scene went from bad to worse when we discovered the lug nuts were rusted and the spare was flat.

"I'll take the tire to the service station and get it fixed," I offered, hoping to reverse this misfortune. I tossed the tire into the trunk of the Dodge and headed for the nearest gas station.

Good news and bad news followed. The good news was that the gas station was only three blocks from the boat harbor. The bad news? The trunk refused to open—I couldn't get the tire out. Unbelievable!

I shattered the silence of that calm, salty morning when I shouted at the Dodge with a string of even more salty words that I had picked up in the Navy. The key, which had opened the trunk lid just minutes before, refused to turn in the lock. I got madder by the minute as I pictured Annie's dad and the rest of the family standing around the boat trailer waiting for the tire. I finally resorted to taking the backseat out of the Dodge and crawling into the trunk to retrieve the tire, fussing and fuming all the way. With the tire finally in hand, I handed it over to the service station attendant (who, by the way, had been watching this entire ordeal). He fixed the flat tire within minutes and sent me on my way.

Returning to the boat harbor, I decided to spare the family my tale of woe and figured they had enough troubles of their own. The old boat was hauled to dry quarters and cleaned from stem to stern, which included rebuilding the engine. It was then traded in on a newer, larger twenty-six-footer that would serve the family for years to come.

The Dodge proved to be a dependable car (as long as I didn't need the trunk), but after a few months I found myself hankering for something sportier. "There will be plenty of time to drive a Dodge sedan," I told myself. Besides, at age twenty-three, this Navy-veteran-turned-college-student needed something sharper, something that would make a statement. You'll never guess what happened one fine day in March.

What I liked: At least it didn't leak.

What I learned: Make sure all test drives include speeds faster than 35 miles per hour.

BOB BELL

11.

Another Pony

It was a sunny spring day in March 1975 when I was once again bitten by the car bug. This time I had decided that it was high time to upgrade the fleet by getting rid of the Dodge Coronet. We still had the Oldsmobile, but I was ready for a five-speed with muscle and power. It was time to go shopping.

When it came to cars, Annie's philosophy was simple: "You find the car for us and then I'll go with you to buy it." She had confidence in me, though she still couldn't understand why *anyone* would trade a Mustang for an Oldsmobile station wagon.

Car shopping had become a bittersweet pastime. The sweet part was looking at all the great cars for sale and picturing myself behind the wheel. The bitter part was narrowing the field and finding the one that would both "scratch the itch" and fit our limited budget.

This particular search had led me to a Ford dealership in Seattle where I was lured to a dark green "sports" car that seemed to have my name written all over it: a 1971 Ford Pinto coupe. The front bumper had a pretty hefty dent in it, which I had determined was the reason for the low price.

"This is it!" I told myself, sliding into the driver's seat. Taking hold of the steering wheel with my left hand and the floor-mounted gearshift with my right, I imagined myself driving the open road, with the windows down and radio blaring. "Who knows?" I thought. "Maybe this cream puff could even lay a patch of rubber on dry pavement."

SALE OF THE MONTH

I was so lost in my imaginary grand-prix experience that I didn't notice the smooth-talking salesman with the sunglasses saunter up. "Nice car," Mr. Smoothie said convincingly. "Just took it in on trade yesterday."

"My lucky day!" I told myself. "Just yesterday, imagine that."

The test drive only confirmed my hunch that this baby would soon be sitting in my driveway. The salesman in the dark glasses blabbed on and on about the Pinto's economy, sharp looks, and kick-ass performance, while I put the pony through the paces on the freeway.

"I would like to bring my wife in for a look and test drive," I said confidently as we returned to the dealership. I actually felt that I was standing on the threshold of the deal of the century.

"No problem," he said smiling as he reached in his blazer for a business card. "We're open till 10 p.m. tonight. I just hope that it's still here." I flew home as fast as I could, picturing Annie doing cartwheels on the front lawn over the thought of having a Ford Pinto alongside the Olds in our driveway.

There were no cartwheels, but Annie was willing to at least take a look at this wild pony. Mr. Smoothie was ready for us and wished us well on our test drive, as he and his boys looked over the coveted Dodge that we were offering as a trade-in.

The second test drive was much different from the first. For starters, Annie kept pointing out some strange rattles. In an effort to cover them up, I flipped on the heater/defroster, only to be greeted by a plume of white smoke that blasted out from all the vents.

"This isn't the car for us," Annie said flatly. "I just want to go home."

That should have been a clue and I should have listened, but I was fixated on buying this car, and for me there was no turning back.

"Oh, that's no big deal," I replied confidently as I rolled down the window and waved out the smoke. "That can be fixed. Besides, they even said they were going to put new tires on the front!"

Unconvinced, Annie grew even more uncomfortable as we returned to the dealership. Mr. Smoothie was waiting for us and expressed total surprise when informed about the plume of white smoke from the heater.

"We'll have our technicians take care of this right away," he said assuredly as he ushered us into his office. "Please have a seat," he cooed to Annie, knowing that she was going to be a hard sell. "Can I get you a drink? Coffee, tea, or cold soda?"

"No thanks," she snapped, glaring at me and then back to Mr.

Smoothie.

Not wanting to waste any time, Mr. Smoothie, still in his sunglasses, sat behind his desk and launched into a compelling pitch: their technicians would take care of the heater problem and put on new front tires as a token of their commitment to excellence and customer satisfaction.

Annie didn't buy it for a second. She got right to the point. "I don't think this is the car for us," she said firmly, pausing to let the words sink in. "But, I will leave that decision to my husband." She glared again with a look I hadn't yet seen in all the years I had known her. I could tell that this important decision was resting squarely on my shoulders. I was alone on this one for sure.

I looked at her hopefully and patted her knee. "Trust me, honey," I said, trying to reassure her. "This is the car for us." Those were words I would live to regret.

Smoothie was ready to add a little more incentive in an effort to massage the tension. "I've conferred with our manager and we're prepared to offer you $500 for that fine yellow Dodge. What's more, if you buy the Ford today, we can get it into our service department this afternoon and take care of these repairs. You can even take my car, a brand new 1975 Ford, home overnight. Whada-ya say?" He stood and extended his hand to seal the deal.

"Hot dog!" I thought to myself. "These guys are giving us more for the Dodge than we paid for it and will even let us take a new Ford home for the night!" I felt as if I was just about ready to pull off the biggest scam of the year.

"It's a deal!" I said triumphantly, reaching to shake Smoothie's hand. We hurriedly signed some papers and proudly drove home in Smoothie's big new Ford with dealer plates.

BOB BELL

LEARNING TO LISTEN

Annie knew from the start that this Pinto pony didn't belong in our stable, and the events of the following months only proved that she was right. From this experience I would learn the importance of listening to her and trusting her instincts. This pony car bucked from the start and was plagued with one breakdown after another.

Sometimes, out of the blue, it refused to start. All the connections seemed okay, but it just wouldn't turn over. On one of these occasions, I became so angry that I got out and slammed the door, shattering the glass and sending thousands of glass chunks all over the interior. Another time, I was backing the car into a parking space in downtown Seattle when the gearshift broke off at the base and just fell over on the floor. Definitely not a pretty picture.

By Christmas of that year, Annie was pregnant with our first child, Kevin, and we wanted to head down to the Oregon Coast for a couple of days. Because of the cost of gasoline (over $1 per gallon—expensive in those days!) we planned to drive the more economical Pinto. But Annie in her wisdom suggested taking the Olds because it was not only more dependable but also much more comfortable. This time I listened to her, and the trip to Oregon was terrific.

After a few short months, we decided to sell the Pinto and ran an advertisement in the local paper. Not surprisingly, we received few calls and nobody came to look at it. I was beginning to wonder how long I was going to be stuck with this stinker of a car.

One Saturday afternoon, a man who spoke very broken English phoned about the car. He asked for directions to our house, which was at least thirty-some miles away from the airport where he said he worked, so I rattled off some vague directions, certain I was wasting my time. I knew he'd never show. I couldn't have been more surprised when he rolled into the driveway about an hour later.

The pony ran like a top for his test drive. When I mentioned it had been temperamental about starting, he wasn't bothered by it at all. "This be good car for me," he said confidently as he offered full price and paid cash. As he drove out of the driveway I smiled and waved, thinking that I was the one who should be doing cartwheels in the yard.

What I liked: This Pinto pony was definitely sportier than the Dodge Coronet.

What I learned: Never buy a car from a salesman who wears sunglasses indoors.

12.

Silver Spurs

Spring always brings signs of new life and growth as the landscape emerges from the grip of winter. In the spring of 1977, our son, Kevin, was almost a year old and we had just moved into our first house. I was going to college and working in outside sales for a Seattle company. Not long after settling in, we found ourselves needing another second car. At this point we still had the Olds Vista Cruiser, which, in spite of its weak points, was still running strong.

My job in sales also paid mileage, so we felt we could afford to upgrade: the last two "second cars" hadn't fared too well, and we finally decided to see if we could find something brand new for a change. The search ultimately led us one sunny afternoon to another Ford dealership in Seattle, where we fell in love with a new 1977 Ford Pinto Wagon. I felt confident that a brand-new Pinto wouldn't be plagued with all the hassles that we had experienced with the previous one. This one was silver with red interior and had red pin striping down the sides. It came with whitewalls, and the wire-spoke wheel covers added a touch of class. This little pony wagon sparkled invitingly in the afternoon sunshine, and I was drawn to it like a magnet. The salesman was great, too, and I didn't even see any sunglasses.

The ad in the newspaper had stated that this particular dealership was giving away a ten-speed bicycle with the sale of each new Ford. We were hooked on the car before the test drive was complete and could hardly wait to take it home. I asked about the bicycle and the salesman launched into an editorial about how this particular car didn't qualify, but I didn't care. I raised my hand to stop his chatter.

"We came here for a car, not a bicycle anyway," I told him. "Let's move on."

It wasn't long before we were signing the papers and driving home in our first brand-new car. The price, including tax and license, was under $4,300 for this sporty little silver wagon with a four-speed. What a deal! It was May of 1977, and we felt as if we had just arrived at the top of the world—on a Pinto pony.

O CHRISTMAS TREE

Here in the Northwest, many families enjoy heading to the hills and cutting their own Christmas trees as an annual holiday tradition. For a few dollars you can get a tree-cutting permit from one of the ranger stations. The rangers provide maps to the cutting area, and for normal people it can make for a fun adventure.

It was the weekend after Thanksgiving, and our little family loaded into the Pinto wagon and headed up to the ranger station, excited about finding the perfect Christmas tree. We were all bundled up for the adventure, with our thermos of hot chocolate, Kevin snuggled in his car seat, and Annie next to me in the front. When the ranger handed us the map to the cutting area, he added a word of caution.

"Be careful up there," he warned sternly. "We had eight more inches of snow last night, so make sure you stay on the road."

"As if I'd consider off-roading in my shiny new station wagon," I thought. Then he smiled and added, "Have a great time!" Annie and I looked at each other excitedly as if we were on the threshold of the biggest adventure of our lives. The eight-more-inches-of-snow warning should have caused me to rethink our plans. After all, our sporty little silver wagon had never even seen snow or experienced the surefootedness of tire chains, which, of course, we didn't have. As we stood there in the warmth of the ranger station, neither of us had the remotest clue of what the next few hours would bring. If we had any inkling, we would have turned around right then and hightailed it back to the city. Instead, we pressed ahead up the mountain, singing Christmas carols and carefully following the map in our quest for the perfect tree.

The road to the cutting area was actually a logging road that snaked its way up into the hills. There were ruts in the new-fallen snow from the vehicles that had gone before us. Driving without tire chains, I tried my best to stay in the groove and not get stuck. The little Pinto crawled on, trusting the route created by all the big rigs and 4x4s up ahead.

After about fifteen minutes of churning our way up the mountain, we came into a clearing with an area for parking. There was a handful of cars parked there, but the ruts in the logging road continued ahead so we decided to press on for what we thought might be another parking area. This would soon prove to be mistake number two.

It didn't take long to realize that we should have stopped at the first clearing, so we decided to turn around and head back. A word to the wise: never try to make a U-turn on a one-lane road, especially on a curved hill covered with a foot of snow. And no guardrail. In the process of turning around, I managed to get stuck (surprise!). Knowing that we needed help, I hoped that the next vehicle to come along would be able to pull us out. Two hot chocolates later, it dawned on me that there were not going to be any other cars coming this far up the road: they had all parked at the first clearing, the one clearly depicted on the map. For all I knew they were probably all headed home with the last of the good trees.

I left my Annie and Kevin huddled in the silver sled and hiked down the road to find help, which, fortunately, didn't take long at all. There were a couple of guys in a big Chevy 4x4 pickup that looked as if it could pull anything just about anywhere. They readily agreed to come up and rescue the Pinto and my shivering little family. The Pinto was unstuck in a matter of minutes, and these Good Samaritans in the Chevy wouldn't accept anything but thanks for pulling our silver sled back onto the road. Soon we returned to the first clearing, parked, and resumed our search for that perfect tree.

We tromped our way through the snow and found a nice-sized Douglas fir that we decided would look great in our living room. After cutting it down and hauling it back to the car, we enjoyed some more hot chocolate in the crisp afternoon air as we smelled the freshly cut tree and even tossed around a couple of snowballs.

I anchored the tree to the top of the car, and then it was time to head back down the mountain and home for the holidays.

As I drove out of the clearing and onto the logging road, several other cars followed. Before long, I was leading an eight-car caravan that was slowly and cautiously winding down the road that would take us back to the highway. We rounded a curve, crossed a level and straight stretch, and then met our next challenge: coming from the opposite direction was another line of cars on their way up to find *their* perfect Christmas trees. We stopped and got out to discuss the predicament with the other drivers. With no place to pull off, we collectively agreed that each line of cars should move a little to the right shoulder and continue forward, hopefully providing enough room for each line of cars to pass each other and continue up—or down—the mountain.

This tedious maneuver started out okay, almost like a slow-motion game of follow-the-leader. As the driver of the first car in line, I felt like I was leading a band of travelers through a perilous blizzard to safety. It was as if we were on a tightrope, taking each step with great caution. We all knew that one wrong move could spell disaster. We were about halfway through the process when the right shoulder of the road gave out and the Pinto slipped into a deep ditch, leaving the back wheels about a foot off the ground.

All the cars stopped and everyone piled out to see if we were okay. The cars that had been following me backed up the road to avoid falling into the same chasm. Luckily for us, the vehicle that I was passing when the road gave way was another big Chevy 4x4 pickup with a tow rope. After jockeying the Chevy into position, we hooked the tow rope to the back of the Pinto. The driver advised me to start the engine and put the Pinto in reverse as he pulled it back onto the road. Though feeling a little rattled, I complied. I recall sitting in the Pinto, with the driver's door wide open, leaning out and looking back toward the big Chevy that promised to pull us to safety. By this time a small crowd had assembled to watch the drama unfold. With the car in reverse, the rear tires were spinning freely (remember they were about a foot off the ground at this point) and the tow rope began tightening as the big Chevy started to move forward. The Pinto started to move backward, and I romped on the gas in a feeble attempt to help the Pinto pull itself free from the clutches of this snowy grave.

The scene that followed must have been a hoot for all the bystanders as they stood shivering in the snow. As the Pinto emerged from the ditch, I was still leaning out and looking back through that wide open door, and the rear wheels were coming down and spinning wildly through the snow. Within seconds a thick coat of ice-cold mud covered the inside of the driver's door, the window, and me. It looked like a blizzard scene—with brown snow. With Annie laughing in the seat next to me, I didn't know whether to be mad or embarrassed, but I opted for thankfulness to be back on the road for the second time that day.

I hastily wiped off the mud as the Chevy driver unhooked the tow rope and tried his best to wish us well without laughing his face off. Humiliated, I just wanted to get out of there and never see any of these people again.

I reached out to shut the driver's door, which wouldn't close all the way because our Christmas tree branches were draping over the sides of the car. In my haste to shut the door, I reached up with my left arm and pushed the tree branches up while reaching over with my right arm to slam the door. Ouch! The door smashed my left arm against the top of the car, sending a stab of pain throughout my entire body. More of that Navy lingo roared up inside me, but I bit my tongue and tried again, this time rolling down the muddy window and reaching through it to hold the branches up while shutting the door. It was done and I was done: time to get off this mountain and go home. The idea of trudging through the snow to cut a Christmas tree had lost its appeal forever. I've never been back to the mountain.

HAPPY HOLIDAZE

Christmas was just around the corner, and Annie's mom had offered to watch Kevin so we could do some holiday shopping. While we were stopped at a traffic light, a full-sized (everything looks full sized from a Pinto) pickup pulled out of a parking lot and plowed into the passenger side of our silver wagon, jolting Annie practically into my lap. The passenger side fender and door were heavily damaged, which made the top of the door pull away from the side of the car. While I would normally love to have Annie in my lap, this damage to our little car was not a pretty picture. The good news was that no one was injured, and the driver of the truck had insurance and took full responsibility for his stunt.

Though battered, the Pinto still ran okay and we were able to drive it for a couple of weeks until the body shop could fit it in for repairs. It was during this time that I decided to run the car through a car wash. I was ready with a couple of towels inside the car in case the water leaked through the half-inch gap at the top of the passenger door.

I sailed through the water and suds application, followed by a good scrubbing by those big brushes that swirl down the sides and over the top of the car. Then I leaned across the passenger seat to hold the towels up for the next step, the rinse. That's when a kazillion little nozzles jetted water like a fire hose as the car was pulled through. The towels were no match for the force of the water, and the jetted water shot through the opening, completely soaking me and most of the car interior. The attendants looked more than a little puzzled when I emerged from the car wash looking like a drowned rat.

To this day I don't know why I opted to have the car repaired at the local Chrysler dealership (maybe because their bid was the lowest). The repair job was good, but I would learn later that their shade of silver paint was just a hair different than Ford's. The difference in grays was hardly noticeable most of the time, but sometimes on a sunny day when the car was clean, it would stand out.

I'LL TAKE DOOR NUMBER TWO

It was another clear, chilly winter morning in February 1983, which found us in a bigger house, this one a split level. Our steep driveway led down to a nice double garage, each side with its own door. Our little family had grown as Kevin was now six years old and little brother, Mark, was three. The Oldsmobile was long gone, and the silver Pinto had proven to be a very reliable car. This was the *Knight Rider* and *Dukes of Hazzard* television era when Michael Knight always caught the bad guys and his talking car did everything but make coffee. Down in Hazzard County the Duke boys roared around, stamping out crime in their bright orange General Lee. Meanwhile, Mark roared up and down our

BOB BELL

sidewalk on his Knight Rider big wheel. Bo and Luke were our boys' heroes, and they were especially impressed with the Duke boys' ability to crawl in and out of the General Lee's windows. Little did I know that I was about to find out just how big of an impression those Duke boys were making on the Bell boys.

Annie was enjoying her job as a substitute teacher in our local school district. One day Annie was called in to sub, so I stayed home with the boys. My plan was to drive Annie to work so that I could use the car to run errands with the boys. I buckled the boys into their seats, backed the car out of the garage door on the right, up the steep driveway, and turned it around at the top so that it would be headed out. With the engine still idling, I walked back down the driveway to shut the garage door. About halfway down the driveway, I heard a noise behind me. I turned around and saw the Pinto rolling backward down the driveway toward me! It all happened so fast that I didn't have a chance to stop the car before it plowed through the garage door on the left, which was closed.

I rushed to the car and found the boys still safely buckled in their seats. "Are you guys okay?" I asked anxiously as I climbed in to check on them. Mark was speechless, his eyes as big as saucers. Kevin looked dazed. "I was just sitting there and the trees started moving!" he recounted. After helping them out of their seats, I hugged them both and offered a prayer of thanks for their safety. Annie came bursting out the front door when she heard the crash and stared in disbelief at the Pinto that had just attacked her split level, backward no less.

"I must not have set the parking brake good enough," I said feebly. Annie knelt down and gathered the boys protectively in her arms as I turned my attention to removing the Pinto from the jaws of my suburban split level.

As luck would have it (and at that point I really needed some), I was able to drive the Pinto right out of the garage and up the driveway, this time setting the parking brake securely. I surveyed the Pony's damage and found a bent rear bumper, numerous scuffs, and a couple of small holes punctured in the roof. The house appeared to have lost the fight, as the garage door that had been closed was crushed about four feet into the garage.

After regaining our composure and reassuring the boys that it was safe to ride with Dad, we all got back into the Pinto, which was scraped and bruised but surviving after its direct assault on the family home. The boys and I dropped Annie off at her school for the day and then headed to our insurance company to file a claim. I parked directly in front of the insurance office where I could keep an eye on the boys, telling them to "stay put" in their seats.

The young lady at the desk greeted me warmly as she began to efficiently take down the information about our "accident." After the normal name, address, and policy number routine, she got down to the particulars of the case.

"Were you driving at the time of the accident?" she asked.

"No, ma'am, I wasn't driving," I replied, realizing that this was not going to be a run-of-the-mill claim report.

"Well," she continued, "who was driving?"

"Nobody," I replied, watching her become a little more uneasy.

"Was there another vehicle involved?" she asked, looking down at her questionnaire and trying to regain her composure.

"There wasn't one," I smiled, now enjoying this game and anticipating her comeback.

"Well," she said slowly as she laid down her pen and looked up at me, "if you weren't driving and there was no other vehicle involved, what did the car hit?"

"My house," I sighed gloomily, wondering what was coming next.

"Your car ran into your house with nobody driving?" she asked with a hint of compassion in her big brown eyes.

"Yes, ma'am, that is correct," I replied.

"When did this happen?"

"About an hour ago."

"Mr. Bell?"

"Yes, ma'am?"

"Can I get you a cup of coffee?"

"Sure. That would be great."

As she stood up, she looked out the window and her big brown eyes widened.

"Is that your car out there?" she asked pointing out the window.

"Yes, that's the one that attacked my house," I replied, nodding my head as I turned around, stopping in my tracks.

It was then that I realized just how much of an impression those Duke Boys of Hazzard County had made on my sons: there was Mark, sitting on the roof the Pinto.

"Can you make that a large coffee?" I asked politely.

Our silver wagon served us faithfully for another year, which included a move to San Diego. When the time came to finally part with it, Annie and Kevin actually cried as the little silver Pinto rode off into the sunset.

What I liked: Our very first brand new car.

What I learned: Buy your Christmas tree from the local Boy Scout troop.

13.

The Camper Caper

One of the family activities we've enjoyed throughout the years is camping, and we have done a lot of it with our trusty old tent and camping gear. A couple of months before we moved to San Diego in 1983, I spotted a 1968 Ford pickup with a camper on the back, parked by the side of the road with a For Sale sign in the window. It was two-tone with powder blue on top and white on the bottom. I just had to stop for a look. "Wow!" I thought as I peered into the window. "This would be great for camping!" The front seat seemed as big and wide as our living room sofa, and the cab included a CB radio, just like the big rigs. The spacious camper included a bathroom, shower, and comfy bed over the top of the cab. Maybe our days of tent camping in the rain would finally be over.

It was obvious that the truck had been well maintained,

and the price was good too. It wasn't long before it had found a new home sitting in front of ours. Nobody in their right mind would try parking a truck this big on a driveway as steep as ours (especially me with my track record). After all, this was the same house that had been attacked by the Ford Pinto wagon just a few months before. If a rig as big as this ever rolled down the driveway, it would keep right on going clear through the house and into the backyard.

In our fancy new truck and camper we enjoyed some terrific family outings before our move to California. When the time came to head for San Diego, we had arranged for the boys to stay with Annie's parents while she and I drove the truck and camper to California. Our plan was to have Annie fly back to Seattle, finish the moving arrangements, and then return to San Diego with the boys when the school year ended in a few weeks. The truck and camper ran like a top for the trip down the West Coast—until we arrived in San Diego, where it promptly blew a radiator hose. But at least it had the courtesy to wait until we were off the freeway and into a parking lot before it erupted.

THE INVASION

After Annie had returned to Seattle, I moved into a temporary apartment that would serve as home until we could house hunt together when she and the boys returned. I had started my new job, and upon arriving at work one morning something strange caught my eye. As I was getting out of the truck, I noticed a thin black line along the top of the fender. Thinking that it was a scratch, I looked closer, only to find that the line was moving. To my horror, a solid line of teeny black ants marched along the top of the fender, up the windshield post, across the roof, and, wouldn't you know it, into the camper. At my first opportunity I declared war on the ants, taking everything out of the camper and going after the little critters with gusto. I did win in the end, but the inside of the camper smelled like insecticide for the next three months.

Later that summer we rented a house in San Diego and happily settled in. When we weren't visiting Disneyland or exploring Southern California, the camper doubled as a guest room.

Eventually we wanted to use our full-size pickup, so we decided to take the camper off the truck. First things first: I needed to install camper jacks to get the camper off the truck. It was then that I realized that the camper top had not been removed in fifteen years.

I located an RV dealer and arranged to have the camper jacks installed while I was at work. An unwelcome phone call came right around lunch time.

"Mr. Bell?" It was the RV shop technician.

"Yes," I replied, thinking they had finished the job early.

"Bad news for you, Mr. Bell," he replied solemnly. "We can't install the camper jacks as we had hoped."

"Why not?" I asked, not knowing that he was about to unload both barrels.

"Dry rot, really bad dry rot in the sides of the camper underneath the aluminum skin." He dragged on, "These older campers have plywood under that skin that are prone to dry rot over time."

"So what are my options?" I asked, trying to find some solid ground.

"Well," he began, "as I see it there is only one."

"And what would that be?" I inquired, hoping for a miracle.

"Leave the camper on the truck."

So much for removing the camper.

I drove it home where it continued to serve as a guest house on wheels until the need for driveway space exceeded the need for an extra bed. We finally sold it to a retired Navy captain who was looking for a "good used RV." I disclosed the dry-rot details, which cleared my conscience and didn't faze him. He left us with a stack of crisp hundred dollar bills as he embarked on what he called "the ultimate road trip."

What I liked: A camper sure beats a tent.

What I learned: Ants will get into just about anything.

14.

The Halloween Honda

One of the realities of living in beautiful San Diego is traffic and long commuting. It just goes with the territory as so many people desire to live where the sun is always shining and the rolling Pacific Ocean is only minutes away. So I knew that the next car for the Bell clan needed to be safe, reliable, and, most of all, fuel efficient.

It was September 1983 and our search led us to the local Honda dealer where we had fallen in love with the new Honda Accord. These cars were selling like hot cakes, and this particular dealer only had one, which sat in the showroom. The cars practically sold themselves; all the salesmen had to do was sit there with a clipboard and take orders. A Honda dealer's biggest challenge was keeping the fingerprints and nose prints off the windows of their showroom beauty.

THE FIRST HELLO: TAKE A NUMBER

After drooling over the showroom model, we decided to join the throng of "Accordians" and get in line to buy one. The process was too simple. Carlos, the salesman, didn't have to be pleasant or even wear a tie or sunglasses. He was helpful, though, and we had done our homework to determine just which features we wanted on our new Accord. The standard equipment list was long, which made the option list a short one. We had decided on a silver-blue four-door sedan with dark blue interior. We opted for the upgraded stereo system and added pin striping.

"How about air-conditioning?" Carlos asked as he looked over the purchase order.

Being a native of the Northwest prompted my ridiculous response that Carlos is probably still talking about today, some twenty-plus years later.

"No thanks, we'll never need air conditioning," I replied, giving Annie that I'm-in-control-here look of confidence.

"Are you sure?" Carlos pressed on. "It's always a plus at resale time."

"Resale time," I thought. "Here I am waiting in line to *buy* this car and this guy is already talking to me about selling it." I had to stay in control.

"We plan to keep this car forever and won't need air conditioning," I said firmly, trying my best to gain the upper hand.

Carlos looked me straight in the eyes for a moment, probably wondering if he was looking at a real-life moron for the first time ever. He laid down his pen, pressed his fingers together, and let out a long "hmm." We weren't sure what to expect next.

Carlos continued to ponder the options as he cracked his knuckles.

"Okay," he nodded finally, picking up his pen and looking over the purchase order. "We'll need a $400 deposit to get this rolling and get your new Honda ordered."

"How long of a wait is there?" I asked.

Carlos flipped a few pages on his clipboard, looked back and forth between our purchase order and a delivery schedule, then turned back at us.

"Probably three to four weeks," he said with a smile, basking in the glow of yet another sale. "It should be here by Halloween."

"Sounds good," I replied as I wrote out the check.

"Thanks for coming in. We really appreciate your business," Carlos said, extending his hand to officially seal the deal.

"You bet!" I smiled triumphantly as we shook hands. "We are really excited!"

Carlos was already shaking hands with the next customer in line as we walked out of the dealership. It wasn't until we were outside that it dawned on me that we had just purchased our first car without even seeing it, not to mention driving it. Annie, the practical one, was still reeling from signing papers to spend a whopping $11,000 for a car.

"We could have bought almost three Pinto wagons with that," she mused.

"Yeah," I chuckled, "we could really have fun with three Pintos! Too bad they don't make them anymore." I squeezed her hand, appreciating her innocence.

Though I didn't say it at the time, I had moved on—after all, it was 1983 and this was Southern California. I was long overdue for something sporty with a five-speed and cool-looking pin stripes.

"Besides," I thought, "when everyone else is running around with their windows rolled up enjoying their air conditioning, I can cruise down by the beach with the windows down and turn up the Beach Boys music on the stereo.

Unlike the birth of our boys, the Honda arrived on its due date of Halloween, as scheduled. We drove home our new "treat," that sparkling new silver-blue Honda Accord. Life was really good.

WAIT UNTIL DARK

After a year in sunny San Diego, we decided to spend our first vacation in Seattle to visit family and friends. With two active little boys, Annie and I hatched up a clever plan to make the twenty-two-hour drive to Seattle more bearable. We would drive all night while the boys were sleeping. It sounded good at first, but we wondered why other parents only smiled at us when we told them of our summer travel plans.

We decided to leave San Diego on a Friday night after work. Kevin and Mark were in the backseat with our little dog, Larry, a golden Chihuahua/Pomeranian mix. Annie was in the passenger seat as the navigator, I was at the wheel.

It wasn't long before the boys were fast asleep with the dog curled up between them. Annie and I had planned to take turns driving, giving each other the chance to nap between turns at the wheel. But when it came right down to it, we both felt we needed to stay awake to keep the driver from dozing off. What's more, it was kind of fun to be riding along through the dark night with the kids asleep in the backseat.

On through the night we drove. With no more than a few minutes of sleep between us, we were coming to grips with the fact that "driving straight through" was not only a dumb idea but also no way to start a vacation. By dawn, Annie was at the wheel while I had reclined the passenger seat and drifted off for a cat nap. I opened my eyes in a daze and looked across at Annie and then out the driver's side window, where the guardrail seemed dangerously close.

"Watch out!" I screamed bolting upright, fearing that Annie had fallen asleep and we were all about to plunge off a cliff to our deaths. I almost grabbed the steering wheel to wrench us back on the interstate as Annie screamed louder than I had ever heard.

"Geeeeez Bob!" she hissed. "You scared me to death! What in the world are you doing? That was soooo stupid!"

I realized then she was not only fully alert and in control but also nowhere near the guardrail. The only danger in this situation was the lunatic in the passenger seat.

"I'm really sorry, babe—that was totally dumb of me," I said sheepishly, knowing that I had nearly steered our shiny new Honda straight into the Pacific Ocean.

"You got that right, you big dope," she continued, reducing me to a new level of stupid. I squirmed some more, telling her how beautiful she was, and she finally started to settle down. But I knew that driving straight through and staying married were not both going to happen.

After a sound night of rest in the backseat, the boys were raring to go by sunrise. Annie and I were not only short on sleep but also running low on humor. I was glad that the boys had slept through my stupidity and Annie's verbal assault that followed: after all, I wouldn't have wanted them to hear their own mother call me a big dope, even if it was true.

By early afternoon we rolled into Springfield, Oregon, and decided to check in to a motel. Annie was ready for a real nap, and I could have slept right there in the parking lot. Kevin and Mark shattered those plans with another hearty burst of energy.

"There's a pool!" they shouted together gleefully. "Can we go swimming?"

The absolute last thing I wanted to do at this point was go for a swim, but I caved at the sight of the pool and our sons' innocent enthusiasm.

"That's a great idea guys!" I said proudly. "Let's head for the pool!"

Annie lounged in the shallow end while the boys and I played hard in the water. One of their favorite tricks was to stand on my shoulders so I could boost them up high into the air and then they could splash down. This stunt quickly wore out this already-very-tired old man.

"Hey, Daddy!" Mark hollered across the pool. "They have a hot tub, too!"

"Yeah, Dad," Kevin joined in. "Can we go in?"

Time for another executive decision. Knowing these boys would one day be selecting a nursing home for their dear old dad, there was only one answer.

"Sure guys, sounds like a great idea," I replied, catching Annie's eyes and flashing a big aren't-I-a-great-dad smile.

Anyone who's been in a hot tub knows they instantly relax you and soothe those tired muscles. Take an already-pooped-out dad, and you can guess what happened next. The hot bubbling water only seemed to energize the boys and to sap the remaining energy out of Annie and me. Kevin and Mark gleefully climbed out of the hot tub and jumped back into the pool. It was all I could do to pull my tired old butt out of the hot tub and jump back into the swimming pool myself. The ice-cold pool water was a shockingly abrupt change in temperature, one that would probably prevent me from fathering any more children.

It wasn't five minutes later that the boys were talking about how hungry they were, so we got out of the pool, dressed back in our room, and went out for an early dinner.

The boys chose Mexican food, and within an hour our tummies were stuffed with our delicious Mexican favorites. The dinner, along with a glass of wine, pretty much pushed me right up to the edge, so it was fortunate that we were able to make it back to the motel.

When we returned to our motel room, it was still early evening. Kevin had found something to watch on TV while Mark was practicing his trampoline skills on the two beds. Within seconds, I was weaving in and out of consciousness, but I mustered just enough strength to announce, "Time for bed."

Somehow this worked, and the entire family was fast asleep within minutes—well, maybe. We're still not really sure exactly when the boys went to sleep that night, and that's probably just as well.

We awoke refreshed and enjoyed the rest of the vacation, having the time of our lives and making memories that are still with us today.

THE LAST GOODBYE

The Honda served us well with years of dependable transportation. On July 4, 1988, the odometer rolled over to 100,000 miles as we crossed the Coronado Bridge in San Diego. As soon as we had crossed the bridge, we pulled over and celebrated with a bottle of sparkling cider. The picture of Kevin and Mark sitting on the hood offering a toast is etched in my memory for keeps.

As the years passed, our family grew and the boys were joined by our "San Diego bonus," a beautiful little sister we named Kristen. The months turned into years, which included a move back to the Pacific Northwest. The Honda rolled on mile after mile and even survived both boys learning to drive.

With the two boys fast becoming young men, the Honda roared past the 200,000 milestone with another bottle of cider. We finally gave it to Kevin when he moved out, and the little Honda continued its faithful service long after the speedometer cable broke at well over 250,000 miles.

All good things must come to an end, and the Honda was no exception. While driving the Honda to work one morning, Kevin was broadsided by a Ford pickup, which spun the little car around like a top. Fortunately, Kevin and his passenger suffered only scrapes and bruises, but it was the end of the line for the Honda.

The last time I saw it was in the junkyard, where I went to fetch a couple of Kevin's tools—and say goodbye. I ran my hand over the once-shiny silver-blue roof, now faded from years of California sun and lined with new wrinkles from the accident. The sad little Honda sat there twisted, and I felt that I was bidding farewell to a trusted old friend. As I gazed in the shattered windows at the dark blue seats littered with chunks of glass and wreckage debris, my mind was flooded with memories that took me all the way back to Carlos in San Diego. It had been a great ride, even without air conditioning.

What I liked: The sparkling cider toast by the side of the road at 100,000 miles.

What I learned: Air conditioning is always worth it.

15.

Airborne!

An incident that happened in May 1987 deserves a chapter all its own. This event changed forever my perspective on life, love, and the things I had taken for granted.

One Saturday evening, Annie and I were leaving a lively party at about midnight. Annie was five months pregnant with our daughter, Kristen, and we were eager to get home and rescue the sitter who had spent the evening with our two boys.

"Not much traffic out here at this hour," I commented to Annie, chuckling that with a pregnant wife and two active boys, our household was usually fast asleep by 10 p.m.

We were driving along at about 70 miles per hour in the interstate's northbound lanes, which were elevated about 30 feet higher than the southbound lanes with a steep grassy slope as the median.

I glanced in the review mirror and noticed a lone pair of

headlights a long way behind us. Within seconds the vehicle was gaining on us. I turned on the blinker light to move into the right lane next to us. Then I glanced back into the mirror and saw the terror of my life.

The headlights of the speeding vehicle suddenly veered to the left. I quickly turned to look out of my driver's side window in time to watch the beige Toyota pickup fly off the freeway and go airborne down into the southbound lanes.

"That truck just flew off the freeway!" I shouted as I slammed on the brakes and slid onto the shoulder. "I gotta go!"

I pulled the trunk release, told Annie to stay put, and then grabbed two road flares from the trunk. From the top of the embankment I could see that the truck had rolled several times but was now sitting upright, alone in the middle of the southbound lanes. But from my vantage point I could also see four lanes of vehicles rapidly approaching.

Sprinting down the bank, I lit both flares and began waving them wildly as I stood between the crumpled pickup and the oncoming rush of vehicles. I heard the terrifying sound of tires screeching and semi trucks grinding their gears to rapidly downshift. There was a flash of brown as a car skidded in front of me, hit the pickup, and then spun around onto the outside shoulder of the southbound lanes. Then more tires screeched and horns blared as this onslaught of cars and trucks skidded around to avoid the disaster.

THE SCARE OF MY LIFE

A man in a plaid shirt approached from somewhere and asked if he could help. I gave him the flares and told him to continue waving them while I walked backward to the crumpled Toyota to check on its occupants. Keeping my eyes on the southbound traffic, I edged back toward the Toyota, aware of the smell of burning rubber, gasoline, and alcohol.

When I reached the Toyota, I took one last glance at the southbound lanes to make sure I wasn't going to be the next victim. The coast was clear, so I turned and looked into the crumpled cab. A knot grew in my stomach. The cab was empty.

LIFELINE

I frantically searched for the occupants—and that's when I saw him. A body was lying about 30 feet away in the southbound lanes. I ran toward it and found a large, middle-aged man covered in blood, with a severe gash across the top of his head. As fast as I could I knelt beside him to check his vitals. He was breathing but started screaming and flopping around like a fish in the bottom of a boat. I put my head near his and tried my best to soothe him. The smell of alcohol was so intense that I wanted to heave.

"You've been in a very bad accident and need to lie still," I said with a calmness in my voice that I've never heard before or since. "I am here for you and help is on the way." He continued to scream and shudder. By now I was gently holding his head between my hands to keep him still. I said a quick prayer for him—for both of us—and repeated my words over and over again.

He began to relax as I reassured him that help was on the way. Other drivers who had stopped rushed to our aid, one with a blanket and another, an angel in a blue dress, who said she was a nurse.

Finally, sirens in the distance grew steadily louder until the entire scene was engulfed in emergency vehicles and seemingly thousands of multicolored flashing lights.

Paramedics arrived and took over, stabilizing this lone driver with a neck brace, delicately loading him onto a gurney, and then settling him into the waiting ambulance, which screamed off into the night. By now the entire scene was swarming with police and fire personnel.

A state patrolman approached me to ask questions. We walked back to his police cruiser, and he took notes as I related the details of the past hour. When he was finished, he handed me some gauze and sanitary wipes from his first-aid kit.

"You might want to clean yourself up a bit," the trooper said. "You've got a lot of blood on you."

I hadn't realized that my bare arms and short-sleeved shirt were covered in blood. But it wasn't my blood: it was the blood of the man who had lain crumpled and broken on the interstate.

"Your swift actions saved a man's life tonight," the trooper continued. "And more than that," he added, "what you did also prevented a serious accident for one driver from involving the lives of many other innocent drivers out here tonight. Thank you. We all thank you."

All I could do was nod my head in agreement until I could find my voice.

"Can I leave now, sir?" I asked quietly, suddenly wanting to run to the arms of my lovely Annie.

"Yes, you can go," he replied, extending his arm to shake my hand. "We have your name and phone number should we need to contact you for anything. Thanks again."

I glanced back up the hill and saw Annie, standing at the top.

After making my way up the hill, I pulled her close and she nestled into my arms.

"I was so scared," she said as she looked up in my eyes. "Are you okay?"

I was numb, unable to tell if what had just transpired was real or a dream.

"Yes, baby," I said as I pulled her close. "I'm fine. Let's go home."

As we drove home in silence, the images of the past hour kept replaying in my mind like reruns of a gruesome nightmare: the flying truck, the empty cab, the man who lay screaming in the freeway, that horrible gash, the alcohol, the sirens.

It wasn't until after I had returned from taking the babysitter home and had crawled into bed with Annie that the magnitude of this experience began to grip me. As I lay there listening to Annie breathing deeply beside me, I held her close and thought about the new life that was growing inside her. What a stark contrast to the gruesome scene we had witnessed only hours before on that dark stretch of the interstate. We were safe and we had each other. Alcohol had once again threatened to take another life, and I shuddered to think that it could have been me, or Annie, or even our unborn child. As I finally drifted off to sleep, I knew that I would never be the same.

What I liked: Knowing that I saved a man's life.

What I learned: Road flares are worth their weight in gold in an emergency.

16.

Along Came Saturday

It was in the mid-1980s in Southern California. As our family was growing so was our need for a second larger car. The minivan craze was on, and with the way that people were lining up to buy them, I couldn't help but wonder if Carlos the Honda salesman had switched models and was now taking orders for this hot new commodity.

Though the minivan was sure to be a great success, we needed something that would haul more and cost less, so we decided to look for a good used station wagon. The search proved not only tiring but also frustrating as it seemed that everything we looked at was priced for the two-income lifestyle and out of our meager single-income range. And then along came Saturday.

After a morning of running errands, I was returning home on the freeway when I spotted what was destined to become the newest chapter in our collection of fine cars. Cruising by on the Southern California interstate doesn't allow much time for more than a glance, but I did manage to note that this beauty was waiting for me in a trailer park. I turned off at the next exit to backtrack for a closer look.

Winding through the side streets finally led me to the small trailer park that housed an assortment of single-wide mobile homes, all nicely kept with tiny lawns and pots of colorful flowers. It didn't take long to locate the car, a dark brown 1971 Mercury Marquis station wagon. This beauty was all stock (but then aren't they all?) and had the fake wood grain on the sides. The handwritten sign in the window provided a phone number and price tag of $750, certainly much more in my ball park. Peering in the window revealed dark brown vinyl seats with no signs of wear and tear.

I found a nearby phone booth and dialed the phone number. After a few rings an elderly lady answered, and I quickly discovered that she and her late husband had purchased the Mercury brand new back in 1971. She promised to meet me at the car in just a few minutes.

When I returned to the car I looked around and spotted the elderly car owner, moving slowly with the aid of a cane. She greeted me warmly and introduced herself as Winnie.

"We bought this car brand new," she told me again with a twinge of a southern accent, "and my husband always kept it up real nice, yes, real nice!"

"Yes, ma'am," I replied politely, already liking this sweet lady. "It does look like you folks have taken good care of this car."

"My husband passed on a couple of years back," she said sadly, "and I never did drive much. Besides, it's just too darn big for me."

Winnie gazed fondly at the Mercury and smiled.

"Do you have a family?" she asked, handing me the keys.

"Oh, yes, ma'am," I responded. "We have two boys, and my wife is pregnant."

"That's so nice," she said with a twinkle in her eyes, smiling again. "So you could use a big car like this one I bet."

"Yes, ma'am," I replied warmly. "Could I take it for a drive?"

Sensing a bit of hesitation, I continued. "Maybe you would like to take a ride around the block in your car?"

Winnie liked this idea and I opened the passenger door for her to get in.

"Well, thank you so much," she said warmly as she slowly got into the front seat. "You are so polite, such a gentleman."

The Mercury started right up and sounded smooth as we backed out of the parking space. But once we started moving, it didn't take long at all to notice a problem: the front end of the car seemed to wobble with kind of a flat tire sensation.

"I wonder what that is all about," Winnie pondered out loud as she continued. "It did that the last time I drove it and I thought it was me."

"Maybe one of the rims is bent or it needs to have the front end aligned," I suggested, sounding like an automotive specialist.

"A front end what?" Winnie inquired, not having a clue about my diagnosis.

I soon realized that nailing Jello to a tree would be easier than trying to describe a front-end alignment to this dear lady. Deciding to cut the test drive short, I found myself wanting to buy the car despite the obvious defects in the front end.

I rationalized all the reasons why I should buy the Mercury.

"An alignment or bent rim wouldn't cost that much," I thought to myself. "Besides, everything else seems to be working fine."

Winnie must have figured I wasn't interested as we made the short drive in silence back to the mobile park.

I parked the car and turned off the engine. I was ready to make an offer.

"Would you take $700 for it, considering the problem in the front end?"

"Well," she began cautiously, "that would be okay. Yes I will."

Realizing that I had just committed myself to spend 700 bucks without even consulting Annie, I had to think fast.

"I'm sure it will be okay, but I would like to double check with my wife, so could I give you a deposit to hold it for us?" I asked.

"That'll be just fine," Winnie replied, obviously pleased with my decision to consult Annie on the deal. "And no need for a deposit, I trust you."

Annie stayed calm during her first wobbly ride in the Mercury, as I had convinced her that the problem was a small one. Winnie's eyes danced as she counted out the stack of fifty dollar bills.

On the way home we dropped off the car at the local tire store for an official diagnosis, hoping that the problem wouldn't cost a bundle to fix. Less than an hour later the tire store manager phoned.

"Your car is ready to go," he began. "The steel belt on the right front radial has separated so we just put on the spare and it rides really smoothly."

This welcome news only got better when he added that there would be no charge for the tire change. I knew where I would buy our next set of tires. A couple of weeks later I returned to the same store to do just that, laying down several hundred dollars for new tires and a set of sporty chrome rims. The Merc really sparkled after a good wash and a coat of wax, and it drove like a dream. I often thought that if Lincoln made a station wagon, this would be it.

RUNNING ON VAPORS

"The wagon is low on gas," Annie informed me one evening as she was relating the day's events on the home front.

"I'll go get some after we have dinner," I responded, not realizing that Annie's definition of *low* was different than mine.

Our house sat at the bottom of a long, steep hill with a curve. I had only just backed out of our steep driveway when the engine started to sputter. The gas gauge needle pointed to the far left of empty, and I knew then that we were running on vapors. The engine roared to life once the car was on level ground, so I hoped there was enough gas to make it to the gas station, which was all up hill from here. I knew I would never make it up the hill if I tried to drive forward. Considering my limited options, I decided that backing up the hill would be the only way to go. "After all," I rationalized to myself, "if I run out of gas or see someone coming, I can just coast back down the hill and into the bottom of the driveway. Besides, it's dark outside and the neighbors won't even know."

With my left hand on the steering wheel and my right arm over the seat, I looked out the rear window and romped on the gas. The Mercury roared backward up the hill and around the curve with a vengeance. Luckily for me (and for them), all the normal people were off the road and home eating dinner during my daredevil stunt. Once on the level at the top of the hill, I spun the mighty Merc around and made it to the gas station some four blocks away in record time. It was as if I was rolling into victory lane as the Merc coasted into the gas station on fumes. Although I was beaming with pride at my automotive know-how, I decided not to disclose my strategy with the burly logger-type giant filling his old truck at the gas pump next to me. I mean, sometimes you just need to keep things to yourself.

DEAD OR ALIVE

After a couple more years of faithful service, I was ready to spice up our fleet, so I put the Mercury up for sale. I was already eyeing another vehicle, but the Mercury had to go first. There weren't many calls at first, but then along came Saturday: the phone rang with the first caller to show any genuine interest. Ralph asked so many questions you would have thought he was making a multimillion dollar investment in fine gems rather than buying our classic wagon, which was up for grabs at a measly $1,800.

The first hurdle was cleared when Ralph agreed to come and take a look at the Mercury. I felt as if I had just won the first round on Jeopardy. When he arrived, he walked slowly around the car several times before even approaching the house. I finally went out and cheerfully introduced myself, trying to tone down my glee at seeing a real-live prospect. Ralph was very serious and kept writing notes in a little spiral notebook. He lowered himself on hands and knees to look under the car and then lay down on his back to squeeze underneath it.

When he was ready to check the inside, I was beginning to wonder if this was turning into an all-day affair. Ralph sat on both sides of the front seat then repeated this process for the backseats. Sliding back into the driver's seat, Ralph took hold of the steering wheel and stared out over the long hood. He fiddled with the tilt wheel, adjusted the seats and mirrors, and finally turned the key in the ignition.

The mighty Mercury roared to life, ready to burn some serious asphalt. But the Merc wasn't going anywhere just yet. It sat there in idle mode for the next half hour while Ralph checked the radio, the heater, the air-conditioning, and every light bulb inside and outside the car. I had never seen such a thorough exam. This episode was beginning to take on a bigger chunk of my Saturday than I had planned. But because Ralph was the only person to show any interest in this classic wagon, I decided to wait patiently.

"We're ready for a test drive," Ralph announced sternly as he buckled his seat belt. He then adjusted the mirrors and carefully scanned the instrument panel with the detail of an airline pilot during a preflight check. As Ralph gradually guided the Mercury away from the curb, I observed an intensity and determination on his face that I had never seen before. Goosebumps followed as we drove out of the neighborhood and headed for the freeway. My imagination started to wander, and I couldn't help but wonder if I would ever see my family again.

Once on the freeway, Ralph continued to put the Mercury through its paces. His stern demeanor seemed to announce "nobody say a word" as he intently listened to every sound the Mercury uttered. The ride was smooth as the Merc floated along the interstate, but I was beginning to wonder if Ralph was ever going to turn around. The right side of my brain was working overtime as I thought about being robbed, beaten, and left to die along the road while this maniac raced off in my Mercury.

By the time Ralph finally exited the freeway and roared to the end of the exit ramp, I was breaking into a cold sweat. Without saying a word, he turned left at the end of the exit ramp and drove back across the freeway, turned left again, and stopped in the middle of the road at the top of the freeway on-ramp.

"This is it," I thought to myself, fully expecting Ralph to pull out a gun and blow my head off. I nervously glanced over and was relieved to see that he had both hands on the wheel, but why was he staring so intently over the hood? We sat there in the middle of the road for only a few minutes, but it seemed more like hours. I found myself feeling sorry for anyone who might innocently pull up behind us to get on the freeway. "What if they honk or pull a gun on us?" I wondered, growing increasingly uneasy.

And then it happened. Ralph slammed the gas pedal to the floor and kept it there as the mighty Mercury lurched forward and sped down the on-ramp. Faster and faster we went onto the freeway like a speeding locomotive, as the speedometer climbed past 75 miles per hour, then 85, and on past 90. Winnie would have had a heart attack if I had ever tried such a stunt on my test drive. When the speedometer neared 95, I had finally found my voice and was ready to forgo any potential sale and tell this moron to slow down. Ralph must have sensed that either the Merc or his passenger were ready to blow a circuit because he promptly took his foot off the gas and allowed the mighty Mercury to slow down to 70 miles per hour, much more manageable and in line with all the other drivers that Saturday afternoon.

The ride back to our house was downright boring compared to the first half of the test drive, although I was still eager to use the restroom when we drove up in our driveway. I'd already made up my mind that Ralph wasn't interested in my classic Mercury at all, and this had just been a big waste of time.

"I'll take it," Ralph announced flatly. "Full price." He extended his hand to shake and seal the deal.

I almost passed out and decided that Ralph was not such a moron after all.

"Sure," I managed to mumble as we shook hands in agreement.

Ralph proceeded to lay down a stack of one hundred dollar bills on the kitchen table as I signed the title while attempting to make small talk. He actually smiled as we shook hands again and asked if he could leave his car at our house and come back for it later.

I nodded, and before I could say a word Ralph was backing the Mercury out of the driveway. My mind started to race again, and I wondered if his car might well be stolen or have explosives hidden in the trunk. I shook my head and decided to go with the flow.

I was relieved when Ralph and a friend returned to retrieve his car a couple of hours later. Ralph seemed genuinely pleased as he backed the Mercury down our driveway for the last time, and I waved as they disappeared around the corner. I was just happy to make over 1,000 bucks on a car that we had driven for well over two years.

"Maybe I should go into the car business," I smiled to myself. "With this kind of luck I could make a bundle and not even need to wear sunglasses." The mighty Mercury had been a great car for us, but now that it was gone it was time to make my next move.

What I liked: A real highway cruiser.

What I learned: Always take a little extra time with elderly folks.

17.

Repeat Performance

It was the fall of 1988 and I had determined that my next vehicle was going to be a pickup. Not just any pickup: I had my heart set on a 1988 Toyota with an extended cab. Knowing that the body styles were going to be different for the 1989 models, I was especially fond of the styling on the 1988 models and hoped that I could find just the right truck. During a Friday lunch hour, I decided to visit the local Toyota dealer to see what I could find. Wes, the salesman, greeted me warmly. I mentioned my search for a new "outgoing" model, and he was ready with a question.

"Ever considered a 4x4?" he asked.

"Not really," I responded, shaking my head, "too expensive."

"Well," he continued, "we're having a sale this weekend on all of our remaining 1988 4x4 pickups. Check them out."

He pointed to a row of shiny new 4x4 pickups that seemed to be calling me over for a closer look. None had the extended cab, but they all looked really sharp. One silver-blue model especially drew me in; when I sat behind the wheel, I fell in love. I knew I had found my new truck.

"The sale starts tomorrow at 9 a.m." Wes said smiling, confident that he had a live one on the line. He was reading me like a book as he extended his hand, somehow knowing that my lunch hour was just about over. He knew I was hooked and that I needed to get back to my "important" job, the one that paid me good money so that I could spend it on one of his trucks. What a pro.

"I'll be here," I replied, shaking his hand. "See you first thing in the morning."

Later that afternoon I shared my good news with Annie. Not only was she excited, but she also agreed that the truck-buying expedition would be a good Saturday morning adventure for eight-year-old Mark.

Mark was thrilled with the idea and ready to go bright and early the next morning. We even had time for breakfast at the local McDonald's and still made it to the Toyota dealership by 9 a.m. straight up. Wes was there, as promised, and he extended a special greeting to Mark, who was pleased to be in on the big purchase. His eyes danced excitedly as he gazed at the lineup of eight shiny contenders for a place in our garage.

"Tell you what, son," I began, putting my hand around his shoulder. "One of these trucks belongs in our driveway," I said kneeling beside him. "How about if you look them all over and decide which one it should be?"

"Really, Dad?" he asked excitedly. "*Any* one of them?"

"That's right, Son, you choose."

BOB BELL

Being the live wire that he was, Mark didn't waste a second. He immediately took charge and carefully looked over every one of the eight trucks—each one seemed to be saying "Pick me! pick me!" I admit part of me hoped he would pick the silver-blue one that I had drooled over the day before, but the look on his face reminded me that this was Mark's choice entirely.

"That one," he said, confidently pointing to a snazzy little 4x4 decked out in charcoal gray with a light gray decal on the side. When we climbed in for a test drive, it was clear that our search was over.

After the test drive and some relatively painless negotiation, we sealed the deal with Wes without having to go above our price limit. We were both pleased: I was happy to finally find our perfect truck, and Mark was proud to have a key role in the process.

The little truck was an instant hit with the entire family, and a few weeks later we decided to add a canopy. It didn't take long at all to realize that the selection of canopies was far greater than we could have imagined. We settled on a custom-fit style that perfectly matched the cab. After adding an alarm and stereo system, we were set for years of reliable service (or at least until another case of new-car fever came along).

A couple of years later found us once again missing the roominess of the station wagon (big sigh). Minivans were still the rage, and with both boys in little league, we knew we needed a larger vehicle. It was tough for me to come to grips with the prospect of selling the little truck, but our growing family needed more space for hauling little league teammates and all their equipment.

The Toyota sold in a heartbeat. I couldn't tell Annie about the lump I had in my throat as I was cleaning out the truck the day the new owner showed up with the check. She would think I was crazy for sure. But for me it was like parting with a member of the family. On the other hand, the new owner, Wally, seemed to like cars as much as I did, which eased the pain of letting it go. As I handed Wally the keys, I wished him well and asked him to call me if he ever decided to sell it. He promised that he would and waved as he backed the truck out of our driveway.

The Toyota's replacement was a 1986 Chevy Caprice wagon that seemed mammoth compared with the little truck. Although we needed the roominess at this time in our lives, I still missed the little truck. The Chevy hauled us through two seasons of little league and family campouts before the transmission gave out and started costing us big bucks in repairs.

Annie surprised me one Saturday morning at the breakfast table.

"You really miss that little truck, don't you?" she asked, sipping her hot tea.

"I sure do," I confessed.

"Maybe you should call Wally and see if he wants to sell it," she continued.

"Are you serious?" I blurted in utter surprise.

"Absolutely," she said smiling. "It would be fun to have it back anyway."

We discussed the pros and cons of such an idea for a while (couldn't have been more than five minutes!) and decided to call Wally. When I phoned him, he not only was home but also remembered me after two years.

After a little small talk, I had to get to the reason for my call.

"So, Wally," I began carefully, "would you be interested in selling the truck back to us?"

"I'd love to," he began as my hopes soared, "but I traded it in."

The words hit me like a ton of bricks.

"You sold it?" I asked in disbelief.

"Yep," he launched into a big song and dance about how he needed something bigger to tow his boat. Blah, blah, blah was all I heard from there.

"What a moron," I thought. Time for a pity party.

"Yes, I just traded it in last week on a Jeep Cherokee," Wally babbled on proudly, revving up for another round of gab about his wonder boat.

By this time I was feeling like I had been left out in the cold on the deal. Why didn't this guy call like I had asked him to when he bought my truck? Didn't he remember? It was only two years ago. I smiled at how stupid it was to be thinking this way and decided to move on.

"Well, Wally," I began, choosing my words carefully, "I hope you enjoy your new boat and Jeep." I secretly hoped that his boat would sink the first time out.

Now the hunt was on. I became a man on a mission. My next step was to contact the Jeep dealer, who told me the truck had already sold. Not about to give up, I met with the used-car manager and told him the compelling tale about my search for the truck and my desire to find out who had bought it.

"Sorry, I can't help you," he sighed, looking at his watch. "We have a privacy policy that says we can't disclose that kind of information."

I tried again to convince him, but he just smiled and said, "Sorry," which really meant "now get lost."

I left the Jeep dealership feeling defeated.

"Oh, well," I told myself. "It's only a truck. Maybe I'll find another one."

Over the next couple of weeks, I checked out several car lots only to find a few very used Toyota trucks. I loathed driving up on the lots where the salesmen would be watching like vultures and then swoop down on me before I even got out of the car. Ugh! I stopped only at the lots that were selling trucks I *really* wanted to see up close. But what appealed to me on the outside always came up short for one reason or another. One look underneath the truck usually revealed dents and scrapes, evidence of some serious off-roading and who knows what else. Over time, my hopes for another Toyota diminished, and the little gray truck became a fading memory. I finally had to let it go and move on.

VIEW FROM THE DRIVE-THROUGH

Several months went by and then along came another Saturday. I had spent the better part of the morning running errands and needed to make a bank deposit. There was a good oldies tune on the radio, so I decided to go through the drive-through window at the bank. I happened to glance at the mini mart across the street from the bank, and my heart almost stopped. There—in living color, parked right by the front door— was a gray 1988 Toyota pickup with matching canopy. It looked just like my old one. Could it be? I had to find out.

With no cars behind me in the drive-through lane, I put the car in reverse and backed out like a wild man. By the time I drove around to the other side of the bank, the mystery truck was backing out of its parking stall at the mini mart. There was suddenly loads of traffic, and it seemed as if every driver was poking along in slow motion. Didn't these people know that this was an emergency? After a blur of tricky maneuvers that must have involved breaking a few traffic laws, I caught up with the Toyota: one look at the rear license plate confirmed my suspicions. It was my old truck!

I started blinking my lights and motioning for the driver to pull over. He must have thought a lunatic was following him because this only caused him to drive faster. I tailed him with honking horn and blinking lights for a good couple of miles before the Toyota driver finally pulled into a parking lot. The driver got out, looking ready for some kind of major confrontation with a mad man. I even wondered if he had a gun or tire iron behind his back.

The driver, Dennis, seemed to relax a little as I rattled off my story about the truck search. He smiled as he listened, probably wondering how many marbles I had lost along the way.

At the end of my dramatic tale, I decided it was time to get to the point.

"Any chance that you would consider selling it back to me?" I asked hopefully.

"Well," he began slowly, "I *have* been thinking of trading it in for a full-size rig."

"Really?" I asked, trying to contain my excitement. "Can you call me if and when you decide you're ready to sell it? I would be very interested in buying it from you."

Dennis promised to call me as I handed him my address and phone number. I was so excited about this turn of events that I forgot all about the bank deposit. I raced home to tell Annie.

Almost two months went by before Dennis called with the news that they were ready to sell the truck. His price was high, but I hoped he had figured in some room for negotiation. I arranged a time to look at the truck. This trip turned out to be bittersweet: It was bitter because a closer look revealed some abuse, wear and tear, and a few cigarette burns on the seats. At the same time, it was sweet to look past its imperfections and think about bringing this little truck back home where it never should have left in the first place. I offered a lower price, hoping to meet somewhere in the middle.

Dennis knew he was in the driver's seat (literally) and probably figured I'd pay any price for the truck based on the way I had carried on. I was thankful that I hadn't tried any cartwheels.

"No," he scowled. "My price is firm."

What a blow. Now I was torn: I really wanted the truck, but I wasn't about to sell the farm to get it. It was time to take a stand.

"Sorry," I replied, "that is just way more than I can afford." Our difference in price was about $1,000, but it might as well have been $100,000. One of the hardest things I'd ever done was to thank him for his time and then turn to leave. I made it to the front door and then turned back to Dennis and his wife.

"I'd really like to buy my old truck back, so please call me if you ever change your mind about the price." With that I turned and made the long walk outside, passed the little truck on the way to my car, and headed for home.

Annie was sad for me, but she also tried to help me look on the bright side (which is something that I just love about her).

"If it's meant to happen, it will happen," she said with a warm smile as she came close for a kiss. "He knows how much you want your truck back."

BARBECUE SURPRISE

A month or so later I was barbecuing on the deck when the phone rang. Annie went in the house to answer the phone, then returned and handed it to me. "Someone for you," she said.

"Hello?" I asked, not having a clue of what I was about to hear.

"Hi, Bob," came the reply. "This is Dennis . . . with your old truck."

I almost dropped our sizzling evening entree right there on the deck.

"Yeah, hi, Dennis," I mumbled once I found my voice.

"Hope I'm not catching you at a bad time," he continued, "but the wife and I have been talking and we think it's cool that you want your old truck back so much. We'll sell it to you for your price if you still want it."

I could hardly contain myself and thought again about the cartwheels.

"Oh, that's so cool! Yes, we would like that very much," I said excitedly, silently mouthing, "The truck! The truck!" to Annie, who broke into a huge smile when she caught on.

Within a week the little truck was back in our driveway, and I couldn't have been happier. A couple of the neighbors were more than a little puzzled, and one of them even inquired.

"Hey, Bob, didn't you used to have a truck just like that a few years ago?"

I just smiled, sighed, and shook my head. "Sure did—it's a long story."

Later that fall, Mark (who was now fifteen) and I enjoyed a "guy's night out" at the annual auto show in Seattle. For fun I entered a raffle to win $1,000 cash, sponsored by our favorite local oldies station. The lucky winner was going to be announced on the air the next morning. (This was the same station that I was listening to the day I had spotted the truck from the drive-through lineup at the bank!) As I dropped my entry form in the barrel, I commented to Mark that the only time I had ever won anything was during a magazine drive when I was in high school: I had won ten gallons of free gasoline, which would have been an okay prize, except that I didn't own a car at the time.

The next morning we were listening to the oldies station while loading up the car for a weekend at Whistler, British Columbia. No one was more surprised than I when the morning DJs announced my name for the grand-prize drawing of $1,000! On the drive to Whistler, Annie asked what I was planning to do with the prize money.

"I'm not sure," I began cautiously, fairly certain that she already had it spent on something for the house or the kids. "Well," she began, "I know how much you would like to get some new tires and wheels for your truck, and I think you should take the money and just do it."

"Really?" I asked, glancing over at my sweetheart.

"Yes," she said smiling, "you deserve it and I love you."

A week later I had everything I could ever want: a good job, a wonderful wife, three great kids, a nice house in the suburbs—and a little truck all decked out in new chrome rims and big tires.

BACK IN OR BACK OUT?

My dad (remember the volunteer fireman?) always backed into any parking spot so he could head straight out if there was a fire. He continued this habit right up until the day he stopped driving at age eighty. As for me, I never really gave it much thought and would usually drive straight in. That is, until one early February morning.

It was 1995 and we were living in another house here in the Northwest with a steep driveway down into the garage. It was still dark outside when I came down to the garage, coffee in hand, to leave for work that morning. I was already thinking about the work day as I opened the garage door, jumped in the truck, and started the engine.

"Lots to do today," I muttered to myself as I shifted into reverse and backed out of the garage. With such a steep driveway, I always backed up the hill pretty fast, and this day was certainly no exception. Now picture this: I had rocketed out of the garage in the little truck and up the driveway as usual, when I felt a violent jolt and heard a thunderous crash that nearly caused me to have a heart attack, wet my pants, or more likely a little of both. My steaming cup of coffee had splashed all over the cab, and I was sure that all the neighbors would be racing outside in their pajamas at any second. I got out of the truck and saw it: the right rear bumper of my truck had demolished the left front fender of a car parked at the very top of the driveway. I just hadn't seen it. This wasn't just any car: it was Annie's special Honda Accord. Definitely not a pretty picture for sure, and one that was about to get nastier. After demolishing the fender, my crumpled rear bumper had hooked under the Honda's left front wheel well.

There they were, my Toyota and Annie's Honda, sitting together like conjoined twins.

Still dripping with fresh hot coffee, I was getting madder by the second. Jumping up and down on the truck bumper didn't separate the vehicles, and I was desperate to get out of this mess before the neighbors woke up. I then tried backing the truck up about six inches, and then cranking the steering wheel all the way to the left to see if I could unhook the truck bumper from the Honda's fender and break the cars loose. The plan (almost) worked, but not before pulling off the Honda's front bumper.

By this time the poor Honda looked as if it had been attacked by aliens as it sat innocently in the driveway. I dreaded facing the neighbors almost as much as facing the insurance company. And what was Annie going to say when she looked out the window? It was just going to be *one of those days*, but we got through it. Both cars were repaired, the insurance company didn't cancel us, and to my knowledge the neighbors never even woke up. The only person that I had to "fess up" to was Annie, and she just shook her head and smiled. She's a keeper. That was well over ten years ago now, and I've been backing in ever since.

What I liked: Watching Mark choose our next truck.

What I learned: Backing into the garage is a good idea, even if you're not a fireman.

18.

Take It All Off!

It was the spring 1990, and our growing family needed yet another all-American station wagon for hauling kids, dogs, bikes, plywood, groceries, the soccer team, and who knows what else. I had fond memories of the mighty Mercury and searched the classifieds for another diamond in the rough. My search brought us to a 1979 Buick Estate Wagon with the third seat in the back. The body was straight and the previous owners had purchased the car new. They seemed like honest, hard-working folks who had taken pretty good care (at least mechanically) of the car. This must have been a beauty back in 1979, with its maroon paint and fake wood grain on the sides. But unlike the Mercury, this baby hadn't aged well. The maroon paint had oxidized (from the Seattle sunshine?) and the once-glistening wood grain vinyl siding had faded into a drab shade of tan. Ugh. Two of the four hubcaps were missing, which only added the blahs to this worn-out looking wagon that most people would have passed on.

True, there was work to be done, but the Buick had potential in my book. It was mechanically sound and priced right at $1,800 (I was pleased to drive it home for $1,500). A can of cleaner wax and rubbing compound helped bring out the shine on the top and the hood, but something desperately needed to be done with the fake-wood-grain-covered sides and tailgate. Starting with the tailgate, I decided to try peeling off the wood-grain material with a razor blade. This proved to be down there right next to impossible, so I consulted my friend Lenny down the street who did auto body work on the side. He would know what to do for sure.

"Heat it up and it will peel right off," Lenny said confidently. "It's just a plastic vinyl that gets really pliable when it's warm. Try using a hair dryer."

"Anything beats a razor blade," I thought while hooking up Annie's hair dryer to an extension cord. With the hair dryer on full blast I warmed up the vinyl wood grain and got underneath one corner of it with the razor blade. Lenny's advice was right on target. The vinyl peeled right off, revealing a beautiful maroon finish that had been kept under wraps for the past ten years. It would take a lot of time and hot air (*that* I had plenty of), but the finished product was well worth the effort.

HOT AUGUST FRIGHT

The labor-intensive process of "peeling" the Buick took last priority in our busy household that summer, and by mid-August I was only about halfway done. One very warm August afternoon, a desperate-sounding Annie phoned me at work. "The Buick over-heated and we're stranded!" she moaned. "We're in the McDonald's parking lot and need you to rescue us. Please hurry."

As I rolled into the parking lot some thirty minutes later, I couldn't help but remember that one of my first jobs had been at this very same restaurant location. It was the shortest job I've ever held (three days), and the only one I've ever been fired from, but then that's another story.

My thoughts jarred back to the present when I spotted the Buick and my stranded little family. What a spectacle that was. For starters the Buick looked like a patchwork quilt, with half of the wood grain and two of the hubcaps missing. Three of the four doors were wide open, and Annie had draped beach towels over the side windows to shield Kristen from the direct sunlight. The boys were sitting on the open tailgate, looking like a couple of shipwrecked sailors. The hood was up, and a light plume of steam was still drifting up from the radiator and engine compartment. The huge puddle of steaming-hot radiator fluid under the front end made it look like the Buick had either thrown up or lost bladder control right there in front of the entire lunch crowd. Yes, this scene provided plenty of lunchtime entertainment for the McDonald's lunch rush. What with my shirt and tie, the lunch crowd might have thought I was just a Good Samaritan helping some sweet young thing and her kids out of a jam. What they didn't know was that I had a much bigger stake in this brood. The problem turned out to be a ruptured radiator hose that was easy to replace, and the Buick was back in service within an hour. I was an instant hero, and the good folks at McDonald's even donated a bucket and water to refill the radiator.

The scene of the disabled Buick still freshly etched in my mind only intensified my desire to "take *it* all off" (and by *it* I mean the remaining faded wood-grain vinyl that still clung to the sides of the wagon). But once I removed all the wood grain and invested in a new set of tires and fancy chrome rims, this once-tired and faded old wagon became a real looker, at least for a few other balding, middle-aged old guys like me.

THE DAY AFTER CHRISTMAS

That year we planned a road trip to Disneyland and were scheduled to leave the day after Christmas. Who would have thought that we would wake up that morning to five inches of fresh snow on the ground? My first thought was to postpone our departure, but the whole gang was thrilled with the prospect of seeing Mickey and the rest of the Disneyland gang in sunny California, so there was no way in the free world that they would settle for canceling the trip, snowfall or not.

The Buick was loaded up the night before (something I learned from Dad), and the kids were ready to go before sunrise. Surprised by the unexpected snowfall, I hadn't even considered the prospect of driving in it for any distance with Annie, all three kids, and the family dog. Our budget had no room for snow tires, studded tires, or even chains, and I hoped that the snowplows had already beaten me to the interstate, clearing the way for a clean shot to California.

On second thought, this was the day after Christmas: the snowplow drivers (our little suburb probably only employed a handful) would be home with their little families, sipping hot chocolate or building snowmen. What kind of moron would pile the whole family in the car and head out for vacation in the middle of a blizzard? (In mild Seattle, five inches of snow qualifies as a blizzard!)

Once we reached the interstate, I was relieved to discover that a few other morons had ventured out this very early morning. Maybe they were headed out to the store to buy batteries for all the new toys at home, or more cocoa mix and marshmallows. It really didn't matter to me. The important thing was that there were some other cars out there to lead the way out of town.

As it turned out, this crazy winter storm blanketed most of Western Washington and Oregon, making for a treacherous driving experience that was anything but fun. Road conditions varied from compact snow, to slush, then to clear, and back to more snow. I gripped the steering wheel, knuckles white as snow, to keep the big Buick headed in the right direction. The roadsides and median were littered with vehicles of all shapes and sizes that had spun out of control and were stuck. I felt the Buick start to slide when, at 40 miles per hour, we hit a big patch of ice. I thought for a second that we, too, were about to join the others in the median—a tow-truck driver's gold mine.

After prying my fingers off the steering wheel and spending the night in Southern Oregon, we tackled the Siskyou Mountains early the next morning and began to see clearer roads and warmer temperatures once we got into Northern California. I relaxed my grip as the tension eased. After stopping for breakfast, we rolled into a service station that included a free car wash along with a fill up. Coated with mud, the Buick looked as if it had rolled over a couple of times in the freeway median. The young man at the car-wash entrance stood ready with a long-handled brush and a bucket of hot sudsy water for the prewash before the conveyor belt pulled us through for the "real thing." He gave us a long, cautious look as we drove up for our turn through the car wash.

"Good morning," I smiled, rolling down the window to greet him.

"Morning," he replied as he stirred his brush in the hot sudsy water.

"We're on our way to Disneyland!" Mark piped up from the backseat.

The young man stopped and gave the Buick another long look.

"Man," he mumbled with a slight drawl, shaking his head. "You folks been doing some kind of drivin.'" If only he knew.

We found the end of our rainbow in Anaheim. One of the Disneyland highlights was watching Kristen lock eyes with Minnie Mouse, high atop a holiday parade float. The magic happened when Kristen waved and Minnie blew her a kiss. Time stopped. What a moment. The 2,000-mile wild ride was suddenly worth it all, white knuckles and all.

SWEET HOME ALABAMA

After a couple more years of faithful service, the time came to part with the big Buick. No special reason, it was just time. Besides, an itch for another set of wheels needed to be scratched.

It didn't take long at all to sell the Buick, and the proud new owners needed a rig with lots of room for their big family.

"We're movin' to Alabama!" Earl exclaimed proudly as I handed over the keys to the Buick.

"Wow!" I replied, unsure of what to say next.

"Yesiree," Earl continued with more than a touch of southern accent. "All ma family is thar and we's gonna move on back home."

Annie and I wished them well as they all piled into the Buick and started off.

"That's the car for them," I said to Annie as we waved goodbye to the Buick on its way south. "Lots of room and lots of zoom."

One evening, two or three months later, I answered the phone and my heart sank. It was Earl. I pictured him and his entire brood stranded along the road somewhere with the hood up and Buick parts littered all over the road. Or worse yet, the Buick had suffered some other mishap that would be traced back to me with the help of some sharp lawyer, ready to sue.

"Hi Earl," I began with as much enthusiasm as I could muster.

"Hi yerself!" Earl exclaimed, "How y'all doin'?" At this point I wasn't sure.

"Just fine, Earl," I lied. "What's up?"

"Well, dats good," he continued, "and I jest wanted ta call and tell yer that we made it fine all the way to Alabama!"

I was bracing myself, not knowing what to expect next but ready for the worst.

"Yep," Earl continued, "dis Buick is da best car for us and we jest wanted to thank yew for lettin' us buy it frum yew and yer good wife!"

"Well, that's just great Earl," I replied in relief. "We're really glad to hear that the Buick is working out so well for you."

We chatted for a few more minutes before bidding farewell, and when I hung up I chided myself for thinking the worst. After all, the Buick had really been a great, dependable car. I had given it a new lease on life when I peeled away the old wood grain and added a couple coats of wax. The chrome rims and new tires would undoubtedly carry it for many more fun-filled miles. I thought back to the overheated scene in one of the many McDonald's parking lots it had visited. I thought of my white-knuckled ride through Oregon. I thought of Minnie's kiss for Kristen. What a car, what a memory. Now it was Earl's turn.

What I liked: Lots of room and lots of zoom.

What I learned: Family vacations build memories for keeps.

BOB BELL

19.

Love at First Sight

It was a bright Sunday morning in the spring of 1984 when I first noticed her in a church parking lot of all places. When she came around the side of the building, her bronze skin seemed to shimmer in the morning sunshine. She had all the right curves in all the right places. Her beige top fit snugly, and I stopped in my tracks as I tried to take in all of her beauty. Everything else in my world stopped as I watched her graceful movements. She moved slowly across the parking lot and then turned in my direction. My heart began to race as she approached. She was flawless. She was one fine—Oldsmobile. That's right, a 1984 Oldsmobile Cutlass. This four-door beauty belonged to the Olson family, who attended our church. Once I had laid eyes on the Olson's '84 Cutlass, I wanted to run out and sell my very-used jalopy— the one with half-eaten french fries on the backseat—and anything else I could get my hands on for a down payment on such a gorgeous car. I decided that one day, when my ship came in, I would buy myself one of these fine cars. Maybe the Olsons would even sell me theirs.

My dream of owning a four-door Cutlass went right out the window a couple of days later when I spotted the two-door coupe version. The best had just gotten better. The lines of the Cutlass Coupe were perfect, and I found myself noticing them wherever we went, loving them more by the minute. The Cutlass Coupe had instantly become my new best favorite and I loved looking at it from every angle. Annie even liked the looks of them, and I hoped that one day we might have one sitting in our driveway. Little did I know that there would be twins in our future.

What I liked: One fine day, one fine Oldsmobile.

What I learned: The Olsons didn't want to sell.

20.

Doubles

The '84 Olds Cutlass Coupe continued to be my all-time-favorite car—my dream of having one grace my driveway never dimmed. Almost eight years had passed since I first laid eyes on that gorgeous machine early one Sunday morning. On yet another Sunday morning in 1992, I spotted the next one that would take my breath away: a two-tone charcoal gray two-door 1984 Oldsmobile Cutlass Coupe with a white landau-style vinyl roof and wire spoke wheels. An up-close examination revealed light gray cloth upholstery in excellent condition. The owners, a family who attended our church, had really pampered this eight-year-old beauty; it still looked as if it just rolled off the showroom floor. What a splendid car!

A few months later, I was out running errands when I noticed an identical '84 charcoal gray Cutlass Coupe parked by the side of the road with a For Sale sign in the window. When I stopped for a closer look I realized that it was, in fact, the very same car whose owners attended our church. The $1,500 price tag left me wondering what the catch was. I jotted down the phone number, raced home, and dialed the number. The owner said that the engine was running rough and that he had been unable to diagnose the problem, hence the low price.

"I've tried everything I could think of," he sighed. "It just doesn't have any power. I figure that it must be something major down deep inside the engine."

I test drove the car anyway, and sure enough the rough engine and performance stood in stark contrast to everything else about the car. Knowing that the car could easily sell for substantially more money, I decided to buy it, rough-running engine and all. I just had to see what I could do to diagnose the problem. One trip to our family mechanic revealed the source of the irritation: one cracked spark plug. We replaced all six plugs and bingo: 100 percent performance. What a car! What a find! Annie fell in love with the Olds and enjoyed the comfort, size, and quietness of this well-maintained vehicle. It wasn't long before the car of my dreams had been taken over by the girl of my dreams. Before long, my drive time dwindled down to putting it into the garage, filling it with gas, or taking it on the occasional Sunday drive. It was time to fine yet *another* '84 Cutlass, one that I could call my own. So I started shopping.

GOLDMINE ON QUEEN ANNE

After several months of scanning the classifieds, I found another '84 Cutlass Coupe worth a look. This one was located on

Queen Anne Hill in Seattle, so Annie came along to check it out.

Olds number two was light blue with a dark blue landau vinyl roof and interior. While not as perfect as the first one, it was still in great condition for an eight-year-old car. The owner had taken good care of it, and after a little driveway dickering we drove it home for $2,400. Another great find!

A couple of weeks later I spent the better part of a Saturday washing and waxing both of the Oldsmobiles until they sparkled. Annie emerged from the house to admire the twins sitting side by side in the driveway. It was time for a decision.

"Okay, sweetie," I began, putting my arm around her. "Which one do you want to drive?"

Annie took some time to sit in each of the Cutlasses (and I was feeling very much like a car salesman). After a few minutes of looking them over, she was ready.

"I'll take the gray one, sir," she said sweetly.

"Would you like me to wrap that up for you?" I asked with a smile.

"That won't be necessary," she replied slowly, stepping close for a kiss, "but tell me, sir, does it come with a service agreement?"

"Anything for you, miss."

"Anything?"

"Yep, oil changes, tune-ups, tire rotations, you name it."

"Round the clock, 24/7?"

"Yes ma'am."

"Well, sir," she purred, slipping her arms around my neck, "I just love the idea of having a big, strong mechanic like you available round the clock."

"Yes, ma'am."

"So, big fella," she cooed, pulling me even closer, "how about coming inside and telling me all about your services?"

"Yes, ma'am."

Annie took my hand and led me inside. She got the gray one and I got the blue one. We were well on our way to living happily ever after.

What I liked: No car payments and one incredible service agreement.

What I learned: Dreams really do come true.

21.

A Tale of Two Plymouths

The year was 1941, and when Pearl Harbor was attacked that early Sunday morning in December, an attractive young schoolteacher named Wilma was just leaving a church service in her small Nebraska town. When the news of the attack crackled over the airwaves, Wilma vowed to her friends that if the United States Navy ever formed a branch for women, she would be the first to sign up.

Wilma fulfilled that promise a few months later when she joined as a Navy Wave. She spent the next several years as a link trainer operator, teaching pilots to fly. Her final active-duty assignment brought her to the Sand Point Naval Air Station in Seattle where she promptly fell in love with the beautiful Pacific Northwest, a far cry from Nebraska for sure. When the war ended and she completed her service, Wilma decided to call Washington home. She settled into an apartment with two friends and took a job teaching at a business college in Seattle. But soon love was in the air and her life changed, big time.

It was 1948, and with World War II in the history books, another Navy veteran, Jim, had returned home to Seattle where he resumed his job as a truck driver for a local dairy. He had served most of his active-duty time with the U.S. Navy Sea Bees in the South Pacific, and now he was enjoying civilian life. He had just purchased his very first brand-new car, a shiny navy blue 1948 Plymouth Coupe that, as he put it, was a real head turner.

Mutual friends of these two not-so-young singles wanted to play matchmaker and finally persuaded them to go on a blind date. Cupid's arrow struck right on target as Jim and Wilma announced plans to tie the knot on December 30, 1948.

"But why the short engagement?" their friends inquired of these two cautious people caught up in a whirlwind romance. "Why so soon?"

Wilma was ready as usual with a comeback.

"Jim wants the income-tax deduction," she quipped with a twinkle in her eye.

It was a match made in heaven as this Nebraska-farm-girl-turned-teacher and handsome truck driver became husband and wife. Now Jim had two "head turners," though the Plymouth was trailing and losing ground by the minute. Their first child arrived in December 1949, and the once-glistening Plymouth took yet another step down in popularity. After all, with a new wife and an even newer baby, who had time to wax the car?

Most of my recollections of that '48 Plymouth are limited to a handful of old black and white pictures. The car was usually parked in front of unknown places accompanied by two well known faces: Jim and Wilma, smiling for the camera.

So just who were Jim and Wilma? They were the best parents ever, and that first baby who arrived on the scene in 1949 was my older brother, Scott. I entered the picture in January 1952. My brother and I were both "chosen babies," as Jim and Wilma chose to adopt children when they had trouble having their own. Tough for them but lucky for us as we were welcomed into the family with open arms.

LUCKY SEVEN

After a few years of faithful service, Jim's Plymouth was replaced by a long line of Ford products. The first was the A. D. (Always Dirty) beige 1951 Ford Coupe, which I remember thinking was about the ugliest car I had ever seen in my young life. This was Dad's work car, and he kept an old army blanket spread out on the front seat.

Dad's job at the dairy started early in the morning and ended about when our school day did. My brother, who was two years ahead of me in school, enjoyed a lot of privileges and responsibilities that I would have to wait for. As a second grader, I turned green with envy when he earned a spot as a crosswalk guard: he could step out in the road with his bright flag and stop all the traffic in both directions, holding them at bay while all of us little kids crossed the street. But my brother took this new leadership role very seriously and he was all business.

One bright, sunny afternoon, as the story goes (I heard Dad's version of it at the dinner table that night), my brother was on crosswalk duty by the edge of the road in front of the school. Looking very official, he was standing there with his orange vest, silver badge, and red stop flag. Scott was very much in charge with his patrol duties, after all this was *his* crosswalk. A couple of his friends had sauntered up behind him when, low and behold, there was Dad approaching in the dirty old '51 Ford. Thrilled to see my brother on the job, Dad honked and waved enthusiastically out the window.

"Hi, Son!" Dad called out cheerfully. "You're doing a great job!"

My brother stared in disgust at the old Ford and didn't say a word.

Scott was quick to the defense with his version (a very lame one, too) of how he was so focused on his important traffic duties that he "didn't notice" Dad and the old Ford.

"Fat chance of that," I mused, knowing full well that this old Ford had a way of standing out in broad daylight, especially with Dad blasting the horn, hollering, and waving.

Scott's face had guilty written all over it, as Dad proceeded to rub it in a bit more; and, being the stinker little brother, I enjoyed every opportunity that came along to see my brother squirm under the strong arm of the law: Dad.

BUCKSKIN TAN FOR THE MAN

Remember back in the fifties when the styling of new cars changed dramatically with each new model year? Major changes in design and style were the name of the game for the American automakers, and some of my best memories are of my annual trek to the auto show with Dad. Fins were in, along with chrome, lots of chrome. It was always fun to sit in those shiny new cars and dream of driving my own one day.

In all my years of growing up, it seemed that any big announcements or interrogations always occurred around the dinner table. There was rarely any warning on these occasions as Dad was never one to beat around the bush. So you can just imagine the surprise when he announced one such night that we were going to have a new addition at our house. I almost choked on my meatball, and I'm pretty sure that Scott was so surprised that the milk he had been drinking ended up coming out of his nose.

"Baby" was the first thing in my mind, and I stared disgustingly across the table at my mom, trying to figure how this could possibly happen. (No, we hadn't had our "talk" yet.)

"We're going to get a new car!" Dad exclaimed, smiling proudly around the table at each of us.

My disgust turned to glee as the topic had just turned in my mind from a baby to a car, a far better topic for this lucky seven year old. I bombarded Dad with a million questions about make, model, fins, no fins, and the like. He patiently fielded each one, and we all talked excitedly long into the evening about my favorite subject.

This was 1959 and our "new" car turned out to be a "new to us" 1955 Ford Country Sedan station wagon. The color? Buckskin tan with bright red vinyl upholstery. While this was certainly no Cadillac—no fancy fins—I knew it was going to be a whole lot more fun to ride around town in than Dad's old '51 Ford coupe. We were now a two-car family.

RED, WHITE, AND TRUE

When the big day came for Dad to retire his old '51 Ford, I don't know who was more excited, Dad or me. He wanted a pickup, and his old Ford was getting really tired. I was just hoping that his new set of wheels would be anything but beige. His new ride turned out to be a 1957 Ford pickup with a three-speed stick shift on the column and a wraparound rear window. The color? Red and white with red vinyl upholstery. This truck was a workhorse and served him well for over ten years. Many of my childhood memories include this reliable old truck.

One Saturday afternoon, Scott and I had the task of helping Dad load firewood into the back of the truck. I could think of a hundred other things I'd rather be doing with my Saturday, which caused me to throw harder as I took out my frustrations on each chunk of firewood. One wild throw landed a log right through that wraparound window, shattering it into a zillion chunks. Dad was just ready to toss another chunk of wood, which he swiftly redirected in my direction, and I caught it right across my butt. Ouch! It was all Scott could do to keep from bursting into laughter. I promised myself that I would one day get even.

Dad never claimed to be much of a mechanic, and he relied on his mechanic friends to take care of most car repairs. He did take pride, however, in doing his own oil changes. On one particular oil-change Saturday, I heard Dad fuming in the garage, so I had to investigate. Five quarts of fresh oil were pooling under the Ford as Dad had just realized that he had overlooked an important step in the art of Oil Changing 101: replacing the drain plug. That was the last time I saw Dad tackle an oil change.

BLACK OVER WHITE

It was the summer of 1964 when the '55 Ford wagon gave way to a glistening white 1961 Ford Galaxy with red vinyl upholstery—a nice car and definitely a real step up from the old Ford wagon. Our parents took us to Disneyland that summer in the new Ford, and I was sure, at the ripe young age of twelve, that life just couldn't get any better. That was a summer of firsts: the first time I could remember going to Disneyland, the first time I could remember having french toast with powdered sugar sprinkled on top, and, yes, the first (and last) time we stayed overnight at a rustic old cabin at Big Sur, a small settlement on the coast of Northern California. That first night, when I pulled back the covers to hop into bed, I was greeted by a giant spider that I was sure would suck all of my blood out and leave me for dead. I refused to get into the bed, even after some pretty tough threats from Dad, who by that time was probably ready to leave me to spend the rest of my life at Big Sur with the spiders. Dad ended up sleeping in the bed with the spider while I slept on the couch, which might well have had all kinds of creepy crawlies underneath.

My mom always had a thing for shiny black cars, and a couple of years later she talked Dad into having the '61 Ford Galaxy painted black. It did turn out pretty nice, especially with the red vinyl interior. She took pride in her shiny black Ford and always kept it sparkling clean and parked in the garage.

It wasn't long before I decided that my Sting-Ray bicycle was due for a color change. I settled on metallic blue and purchased the largest can of spray paint I could afford. After all, a paint job of this magnitude would require at least two coats. What's more, it certainly couldn't be done outside, so I decided to bring my bike into the garage for the task. I spread newspapers on the floor, shook the can of metallic blue enamel, and sprayed away, oblivious to the glistening black Ford Galaxy sitting directly behind my bike less than three feet away. Get the picture?

I was almost done when Dad walked in and surveyed the scene. The good news was that the two coats of metallic blue paint covered the bike really well. You can guess the bad news: the overspray managed to cover everything else, including me, the newspapers on the floor, and, yes, the driver's side of Mom's shiny black Ford. Dad had more than a few choice words over that one and proceeded to give me a swift kick in the butt, which I decided had a lot more punch to it than a piece of firewood.

The next few years would prove to be tough on this Ford as both my brother and I would learn to drive. Yes, in this car I got my first driver's license, my first date, and even my first real kiss, which was a whole lot better than french toast with powdered sugar. This aging black beauty finally met its demise one night when I was returning home: I hit a patch of ice and wound up in a deep ditch. The Ford was high centered, with its rear wheels off the ground and nose buried into the muddy ditch. Some people who lived near the scene heard the commotion and let me use their phone. I called Dad and asked if he could bring his truck and a rope to pull the Ford out of the ditch. As I hung up the phone and started for the door, I heard a loud crash outside.

My heart sank as I raced outside and saw it: a shiny new Buick had hit the same patch of ice, slammed into the side of the Ford, and knocked it out of the ditch and into the front yard of the house where I had just used the phone. By the time Dad arrived with the tow rope, I was sitting in a state patrol car, watching

BOB BELL

tow trucks retrieve the Ford from the front yard and haul off the crumpled Buick.

Dad probably could have (or should have) lectured me that night, but instead he put his arm around my shoulder and pulled me close.

"Cars can be replaced, but kids can't. I'm so thankful that you are okay."

I was thankful too, not only for safety but also for such a great Dad.

FINAL FORDS

The next Ford car in my parents' garage was another Ford Galaxy, this one a silver-blue 1969 two-door that arrived in 1970 as a replacement for the battered '61 (now headed for the junkyard). I had just started dating Annie, and it was a treat to occasionally drive her around in the '69 Galaxy, rather than in some of the crates we had previously owned. Besides, all the parts actually worked and it didn't require scraping ice on the inside of the windows.

Dad's '57 Ford was replaced by another red and white Ford pickup, a 1965 model complete with an air horn and lights on top of the roof just like the big rigs. A few years later he traded this truck in on a silver 1977 Ford F-150 pickup with black interior. It would be Dad's last truck—the nicest one he ever owned. He looked good in it and was so proud of it.

BREAK IN THE FORD CHAIN

It was 1983 when Mom inherited a 1968 Plymouth Fury from her cousin Gayle. Gayle had been a widow most of her adult life and had purchased the car brand new in 1968 with almost every option, except a radio. The good news was that this four-door sedan was immaculate and came with very low miles. The bad news in my book was the color: beige.

This Plymouth served my parents faithfully in their senior years, and it was always great to see them drive up together in this grand old car. They were in their eighties and did most everything in slow motion. One day I was driving home from work and found an unusual backup of cars crawling along the main road that led to our neighborhood. The speed limit was 35 miles per hour, and most people did at least 45. My first thought was road construction or an accident, but I soon discovered the reason for the long line of cars: in the lead was a beige '68 Plymouth creeping along at a turtle's pace with its two elderly occupants—you guessed it, Mom and Dad. As they turned onto our street, the line of cars behind them hit their throttles like the start of the Indy 500. Mom had given up driving several years earlier, and Dad knew that his driving days were numbered: he would soon hang up his keys for good.

Their relationship had started in the blue '48 Plymouth and had covered a lot of miles over a lot of years, ending with the '68 Plymouth. When Dad decided to hang up his keys for the last time, the Plymouth did find a new home, this time in our driveway. Yes, Grandpa decided to sell it to our son, Mark, who at age sixteen was excited about getting his first car.

Mark learned a lot from the old Plymouth in the few short

years that he drove it, much of which we would hear about years later. One was that the Plymouth could hold a grand total of twelve teenagers for a trip out to lunch and back to the high school. The old car just wasn't equipped to hold up under the lead foot of a teenage thrill driver and, as a result, made its last ride out of the neighborhood on the back of a flatbed truck for a trip to the junkyard.

What I liked: A bruiser of a cruiser and a great car for a first-time driver.

What I learned: A wise person knows when to hang up the keys.

22.

The White Tornado

I well remember how impressed I was with some of the car advertisements that started coming on in the late sixties. One such advertisement showed a new Ford Galaxy driving up multiple flights of stairs in a stadium to demonstrate durability. I secretly wished my dad would run out and snap up one of these beauties, but that was never going to happen. I knew he would never part with his worn-out '57 Ford pickup and Mom was content with her 1961 Ford Galaxy, so all I could do was dream. The Ford station wagons built between 1965 and 1967 were some other big favorites for me (especially the 1967 model). I loved the lines of these big Fords, especially the chrome grill with the stacked headlights.

When my friend's parents bought a shiny new red 1967 Ford Country Squire station wagon (the one with the fake-wood side panels) I wondered if they might adopt me. But at age fifteen, I was young, naïve, and spent most all of my time thinking of only two things: girls and cars, girls and cars.

Fast forward to 1993 and the picture had changed a bit: I was married and had three kids (two of them teenagers), two dogs, two cats, a turtle, and a nice house in the suburbs with two Olds Cutlasses in the garage. And yes, I'm still crazy about girls (Annie and our daughter, Kristen) and cars.

BLAST FROM THE PAST

It was mid-afternoon and I was on my way home from work when I spotted it. There, parked along the side of the road, was a 1967 Ford Country Sedan station wagon. (The Country Sedan station wagon differed from the Country Squire in that it didn't have the fake wood sides.) As I drove by, I slowed for a peek and to my surprise saw a For Sale sign in the window. I just had to stop for a closer look.

The Ford was white with turquoise interior, and aside from a couple of scratches and minor door dings, the body was straight and in good shape. The white-wall tires looked to be in decent shape, and all four original hubcaps were in tact. Reading the fine print on the sign, I did a double take at the price. Five hundred even—a bargain for a twenty-six-year-old classic!

"Gotta have this one," I muttered to myself, thinking of all the fun we (well, okay, I) could have with this old wagon, truly a blast from the past.

But there had to be a catch, and I couldn't help but wonder if the beast even ran. I jotted down the phone number and spent the rest of the drive home trying to figure out how to spring this

BOB BELL

one on Annie. What would she say?

Rolling into our driveway a few minutes later, I discovered that Annie wasn't home yet. The wheels were already turning in my head: How could I justify buying a car that I not only didn't need but also didn't even know if it ran. I dialed the number and was surprised to hear a pleasant voice and not an answering machine.

"Hi there," I began excitedly. "I'm calling about the Ford wagon you have for sale."

"Yes!" came the friendly reply. "My name is Donald and my dad bought it new in 1967 and it has been in our family ever since."

"Does it run?"

"Absolutely," Donald replied, "it runs like a champ! The only problem is that it has a hole in the exhaust manifold, so it is pretty loud."

"Why are you selling it?" I persisted.

"Well, we've had it parked here at the house and just don't need it anymore."

We talked a few more minutes and I decided to set up a time to drive the Ford, hoping Annie would agree to take a look. Annie had a few things to say about it on the way over for our test drive, but to my surprise she was pretty excited about the prospect of adding this classic to our fleet of aging vehicles.

Sitting behind the wheel reminded me of the sheer size and magnitude of this old wagon. From my driver's seat vantage point, it looked as if the hood ornament was a good country mile out in front. Right away I loved everything about this huge car. The engine roared to life when I turned the key, and judging by the deafening noise, I figured that the hole in the exhaust manifold must have been the size of Rhode Island. The test drive was a blast (literally!) and the Ford had loads of power. A steal at $500!

Kevin and Mark were thrilled when we rolled up in the driveway in the Ford. In their eyes, this car was old enough to be "cool," and they (especially Kevin) considered it a status symbol. Their friends were crazy about it, too, and shared the consensus that the hole in the manifold should remain because it made the Ford sound like a real hot rod. The Ford was fun to drive and a real looker. It turned a lot of heads, though we were never sure whether it was the vintage lines or the loud exhaust sound created from the gaping hole in the exhaust manifold that drew all of the attention.

It was loud and fast and could take out almost everything in its path; thus we named it the White Tornado.

UP CLOSE AND PERSONAL

It was family night and I drove the Ford to the video store to pick up a movie. On the way home I tuned the radio to the local oldies station and cranked up a Beach Boys tune that could barely be heard above the roar of the engine. It was dark outside and I must have been about a mile from home with the old Ford lumbering along at about 40 miles per hour, when I was distracted by something along the side of the road. Suddenly I realized that the car ahead of me had stopped. I slammed on the brakes and all four wheels locked up as the big Ford skidded to a stop in a cloud of smoking rubber, just inches behind the car full of teenagers ahead. The kids in the backseat turned around and looked terrified when they saw the smoking grill of the White Tornado.

BOB BELL

Before long we started rolling again, but the teenagers in front of me kept turning around and staring as if they were being followed by a mad man in a tank. They were right about the tank, but I certainly wasn't a mad man; my heart was pounding like crazy and I was shaking like a leaf at the thought of rear ending a car full of kids.

A few blocks up the road, the car ahead turned right on a side street, and I can still see the faces of the kids in the backseat peering out the window to see where I would go. I wondered why they were so eager to ditch me. It turned out, however, that the side street they had selected happened to be my street, so their eyes only got bigger as the White Tornado continued to follow them.

Down the street a block or so the car ahead turned left into a cul-de-sac, with the kids in the back still watching the roaring Ford. This, too, was *my* cul-de-sac so I continued to follow them. They made a quick turn into the first driveway on the right—*my* driveway. By now they must have either known exactly where they were going or getting ready for a confrontation. I watched as the teenagers started moving around in the car. For all I knew, they were loading guns for a shoot out.

There was nothing to do but to turn the big Ford into the driveway behind them. As I shut off the engine, all four doors of the car ahead opened. Still shaking from the near miss a few minutes before, I felt like a sitting duck before a gang of hoodlums. Maybe they had lured me into this quiet cul-de-sac to get even for scaring the crap out of them. Didn't they know I was scared, too? My heart was pounding as they emerged from the car, six teenage guys in all. I braced for a confrontation, and my only hope was that Annie would hear the gunfire and call the police before these gangsters escaped. And then it happened.

One squinted into the glaring headlights of the Ford and asked, "Is that you, Mr. Bell?"

It was only then that I recognized him, as well as the other five, all Kevin and Mark's friends. Getting out of the car, I felt both relieved and stupid.

"Sorry for what happened back there," I began, feeling more than a little embarrassed. "I sure didn't mean to scare you like that."

All six boys appeared to relax a little once they recognized me and realized that I wasn't going to kill them. Not knowing it was family night at our house, they had actually been on their way over to hang out with our sons. Kevin and Mark came out of the house a few minutes later, and we all had a good chuckle as the other boys recounted the incident and their brush with a mad man driving the White Tornado.

TEMPERATURE RISING

The big Ford continued to run good and was a real hit, especially with all of Kevin and Mark's friends. It would go just about anywhere and haul just about anything. One warm summer evening stands out in my mind: We hauled the boys and a wagonload of their friends to their favorite spot at the river to swim and jump off a nearby bridge into the cool, refreshing water. We enjoyed watching them from our vantage point on the Ford's big hood.

A few weeks later we loaned the wagon to some friends who were helping their kid move into a downtown Seattle apartment. It was a scorching hot summer day, and, with all the moving and crawling up and down the hills of Seattle with loads of furniture, the Ford overheated—big time. But with more furniture to move, no one thought of letting it cool off or giving it a drink. They pressed it to the max, finished the move, and brought it back to our house where it died at the end of the driveway, cracked block and all. It was a sad day and little did we know that the White Tornado had made its final roar.

When I discovered that all of the options for fixing the big Ford were out of my price range, I chose to sell it, hoping that someone would come along and fall in love with it just like I had a couple of years before. We ran an advertisement in the classifieds for the better part of a month but didn't get a single call. Then one day I spotted a sign, "We buy junk cars," and jotted down the phone number. I held out for a few more days, hoping someone would appear at our door to rescue the old Ford, but in 1996 there wasn't much of a market for a 29-year-old wagon, especially this one.

I finally surrendered and called the junk dealer, who agreed to take a look at our classic wagon. I thought that once he saw the car he would realize the potential of pumping some new life into this beauty and offer us top dollar. But my hopes were dashed the minute he showed up with his flatbed truck. This guy had the personality of a dried prune and considered the Ford just another hunk of scrap. That would be crap with an *s* on the front. He offered me a whopping fifty bucks for her in a take-it-or-leave-it tone. Though his fifty-buck offer left me feeling ripped off, I thought of how equally unfair it would be to the neighbors to leave this dead wagon at the end of the driveway indefinitely. I could picture it a moldy green color with moss and weeds growing out of the scum that accumulated on the roof. It was then that I decided to spare this old wagon from such an embarrassing experience. I thought, too, of what the neighbors might do to my house during the night in revenge for parking the old crate in their direct line of vision. After mumbling something about being screwed, I sighed and took the fifty bucks. Within ten minutes the junk man had the wagon loaded on his flatbed. The big old Ford that could once run up and down the stairs of a stadium was carried out of the cul-de-sac on a stretcher for its final ride.

What I liked: What a cruiser!

What I learned: Always keep your eyes on the road, always.

23.

The Bug Collection

Have you ever noticed how some children have a fascination with bugs? They look for them, collect them, put them in jars with holes on the top, and adopt them as pets. Our son Mark had a fondness for a different kind of bug that started right about the time he got his driver's license. These are the VW bug variety with four wheels; Mark has owned a string of them that have come and gone over the years. He looked for them, collected them, and adored four of them that together weave quite a tale.

BUG #1: THE RED ONE

Mark's first bug was a red 1973 Super Beetle that he bought for $600 from a friend who needed the cash. This first experience with a Volkswagen proved to be a real learning opportunity for him. With the help of his friends, Mark became very familiar with the entire car from bumper to bumper: there was always something that needed fixing or rebuilding. He and his friends had stashed an assortment of spare VW parts in our barn that would surely come in handy "someday."

From the moment he purchased it, the starter on this first bug never did work, so Mark would always park his car on an incline so he could push the car or roll it and pop the clutch to make it start. It would seem that most folks would have taken the time to get the starter replaced, but Mark seemed to take this all in stride. He always had a variety of things going on in his life, so he would just smile and say "someday I'll get that starter replaced." He probably had a starter or two in his "someday" pile, but just somehow never got around to it.

One chilly fall evening, Mark parked his bug at the end of our driveway, facing down a slight slope so he could roll it forward to compression start the engine when it was time to leave. When it was time for Mark to go, he returned to the end of the driveway, only to discover that his little red bug had disappeared. He raced down the street in search of his car. He didn't have to go very far, for there it was, nestled in the bushes and trees in the front corner of our property. Because the parking brake wasn't set all the way, his little red bug had decided to take a ride by itself. Lucky for Mark the front wheels were turned just enough to guide the wayward bug down the street, in and out of the grassy ditch, and finally into the bushes (but, thankfully, not into the trees). It was like a game of hide and seek! Annie thought the situation was hilarious and raced out with the camera to snap a few pictures of the bug in the bushes, but Mark failed to see any humor in the situation. Being a good sport, he quickly recovered from his embarrassment; and with a little help from Dad, he had the bug out of the bushes and back on the road in less than an hour.

A couple of weeks later, Mark was driving his bug down a residential street when an elderly lady in a shiny new car pulled out in front of him. Mark slammed on the brakes and veered to the left to avoid a collision, which caused him to lose control of his bug and plow through the brick wall of a new subdivision entrance. Fortunately, he walked away from the crumpled bug with only a couple of scrapes and bruises. The little red bug spent the next couple of months in our garage being stripped for any salvageable parts that could be added to the growing pile of bug inventory out in the barn.

BUG #2: THE WHITE ONE

The discovery and acquisition process for all of Mark's bugs was as unique as each car itself. Every day on his way to work, Mark passed an older white VW bug parked next to a garage. Most people would have driven by without noticing it, but Mark had noticed, and after a couple of weeks, decided to inquire.

There were no For Sale signs posted on the car, and a closer look revealed that it had been sitting there for some time. It was not only filthy but also taking on a greenish color from the surrounding vegetation that was starting to grow over it. Despite this, Mark saw its potential and decided to knock on the door of the residence and ask if the car was for sale. The surprised owner answered the door and chatted with Mark briefly, mentioning that the car hadn't run for well over a year.

"Not a problem!" Mark responded to the owner. "Would you

sell it for $150?"

Once he became the proud owner, Mark installed another engine, and the sleepy little bug roared to life after the successful transplant. But it still refused to move: the rear brakes were locked up from sitting so long. A couple of whacks with a hammer did the trick, and soon the little white bug was sitting alongside *our* garage.

Not long after Mark purchased the white bug, I came home one evening and ventured out to the garage, expecting to see Mark and his friends going about the task of stripping the red bug of its parts. But what I found was a battered old silver VW right where the red one had been just the day before. Sensing that the situation was a little odd, I decided to inquire.

"Hi, guys!" I began cheerfully. "What's up?"

"Hi, Dad!" Mark responded enthusiastically. "We're just getting some more parts off this bug to use on my white one."

Something didn't "smell right" here—anyone who's raised a teenager knows the kind of hunch I'm talking about.

"Sounds good," I said slowly. "Where did you find this one?"

Mark and his friends looked at each other, more evidence that something was amiss.

"Ah . . . well . . ." Mark began sheepishly. "We found it in the bushes."

"You what?" I replied.

"Found it in the bushes," Mark continued, "actually in the woods down off of Lancaster Road."

I was speechless, but not for long. I was going to find out how they had accomplished this feat but was smart enough not to ask them directly.

"Who does it belong to?" I asked, afraid of what I might hear.

Mark looked at his friends again, trying to get some moral support and probably hoping that the old man would get struck by a sudden bolt of lightning.

"It belongs to my friend, Mike," Mark continued, looking at the floor. "And he said we could get these parts off of it and then we'll take it back."

"Let me get this straight," I began slowly. "This car belongs to your friend and he keeps it in the woods?"

"Yes, sir," Mark replied, finally looking me in the eye.

I didn't need to ask any more questions. Mark knew what to do, and when I came home from work the next afternoon, the garage was empty. Mark assured me that he and his friends had returned the silver bug to the place they had found it. I really didn't need to know any more about Mark's friend or why he kept his car in the woods. I had learned that sometimes you just need to let things go. No questions, no interrogation, just let it go.

BUG #3: THE CLASSY VAN

Mark really admired the older VW microbuses, vowing to one day have his very own. That day came when a friend offered to sell Mark a 1966 VW camper van with a blown engine. This would truly be a project car, and Mark couldn't wait to get started. That was in 1998, and it was nothing short of amazing to see what Mark did with this van. Mark began the renovation by replacing the engine with a larger rebuilt engine, and then he kept going, replacing a host of items throughout the van. To this day he keeps it garaged, working on it when he finds the time and driving it on special occasions.

BUG #4: THE GREEN ONE

The last bug in Mark's collection was a 1964 green beetle that he bought for $50. Add to that another $70 for a set of front fenders and he had a car that would last him for the next four years. It ran pretty well and the body was fairly straight—not bad for a $120 investment.

One of the unique things about this bug was the front seat on the passenger side. It looked okay, but the moment you sat down you knew there was a problem: a broken bracket on the right side caused the seat to lean and turn slightly to the right (which was fine if you didn't mind turning your head to the *left* to look out the windshield).

The little green bug ran great, and Mark finally sold it to his good friend Justin, a fellow VW enthusiast who completely restored the car from bumper to bumper. The finished product was gorgeous, and who would have thought that it all came from a tired little car that Mark had purchased a few years back for $50 plus a couple of fenders.

What I liked: Mark's ability to see a diamond in the rough.

What I learned: Some things matter, others don't. Choose your battles.

24.

Huck and Babe
the Blue Olds

Several years after the two '84 Cutlass Coupes had moved up and out of our fleet, I found myself hankering for another one. Once in a while I would glance through the classifieds, but I never saw anything with even a hint of potential. Annie was driving another '84 Olds Cutlass, a black four-door with all the bells and whistles available on a car in 1984. We had started naming our cars, both out of fun and in memory of the old Ford Wagon (a.k.a. the White Tornado). I'm not sure how this Olds had been dubbed Betty, but that's exactly what Annie called her, so it stuck.

While scanning the classifieds one Sunday afternoon, I spotted an advertisement for yet another 1984 Olds Cutlass Coupe. It sounded worthy of a phone call, a long-distance one at that. An elderly sounding man answered the phone and told me that the car had belonged to his brother who recently passed away. His description of the car and its condition convinced me that it was worth a firsthand look. The owners lived south of Seattle, less than an hour away, so I decided to check it out. Besides, it was a nice afternoon for a drive.

Their last name was Busto, and their driving directions led me right to their house. The red Olds was parked next to the driveway. Much to my surprise, another '84 Cutlass Coupe was tucked into the carport: this one was blue with a dark blue top, similar to the one I had owned a few years before. The finish on the red one was heavily oxidized and would need a good detailing, but the blue one just sparkled! This was going to be an interesting visit, for sure.

The Bustos greeted me warmly. I soon learned that they had lived in this house for well over forty years and had raised their children here. They invited me inside and seemed eager to visit, telling me all about the red Olds and the brother who had owned it. By the time I went outside for a test drive, I felt like I had known this delightful elderly couple for years.

When I turned the key, the red Olds fired right up, and Grandpa Busto climbed in to accompany me on a test drive. There were no dents or scratches in the body, no rips or tears in the red vinyl upholstery. Aside from missing a hubcap, the car just needed a good detailing inside and out. It drove smoothly, the price was fair, and I knew that with a little elbow grease it would shine up pretty good.

When we returned to the house, Grandpa Busto asked if I liked the car enough to buy it.

"Well," I began, "I'd like to think about it overnight, but if you were selling the blue one I'd buy it today. It is a beautiful car."

"That's Grandma's car," he said smiling and looking toward the carport. "I don't think she would ever part with it." We walked over to the blue car for a closer look. It was indeed gorgeous and the mileage was really low.

"I can sure understand that," I replied as I got in my car to leave. "How about if I call you tomorrow and let you know either way about your brother's car."

"Sounds good," he said smiling again. "Have a safe drive home now."

Annie was open to the idea of another Cutlass and smiled as I told her about Grandpa and Grandma Busto's hospitality. I called them the next afternoon to make an offer of $2,500 for the red Cutlass. Grandpa Busto was pleased that we wanted the red car. And he had a surprise for me.

"Well, here's one for you, son," he said slowly. "I've been talking this over with Grandma, and she'd like to sell you the blue one, too. Do you want both of them?"

I almost dropped the phone.

"Wow," I said, hardly able to contain myself. "Sure! Yes! But, how much would you be asking for the blue one?"

"How about $4,500 for both of them?" he replied.

I covered the receiver and mouthed to Annie that Grandpa Busto offered to sell us both Oldsmobiles. She smiled and told me it was my decision. She knew that we had come a long way since the fiasco with the Ford Pinto years before.

"That sounds great," I began. "We would like to buy the red one for sure, and I'd like to drive the blue one before we make a final decision."

"That would be just fine, son," he replied warmly. "When

would you like to come back down?"

We arranged for a return visit, which gave Annie an opportunity to meet Grandpa and Grandma Busto, who were pleased to have some more company. Their warmth and graciousness made us feel right at home. Grandma Busto offered us some lemonade and eagerly showed us around the yard. When Grandpa Busto learned that he and I had both worked for the Boeing Company, he had even more stories to tell.

We finally took the blue Olds for a drive, and it handled perfectly. They told us that they had bought it brand new in 1984 and always kept it in the garage. Grandma Busto had indeed been the primary driver and had taken exceptional care of the car. What a find!

WHAT'S IN A NAME?

We opted to buy both of the Oldsmobiles. Grandpa Busto chuckled when he heard that we had already owned three '84 Cutlasses and were about to acquire two more.

Annie had noted that the first three license plate letters on the red Olds were HUC, so we added K and named the red one Huck. The blue one would become Babe the Blue Olds. Betty, Huck, and Babe the Blue Olds. Three '84 Olds Cutlasses were definitely going to fill up the garage and driveway at the Bell house!

PLUMS, POTATOES, AND A BOUQUET

The next afternoon Annie drove me back down to the Busto's so I could pick up Babe the Blue Olds, the newest addition to our "fleet." Annie dropped me off and then headed for home in an effort to beat the rush-hour traffic going back through Seattle.

"I'll be about ten minutes behind you," I told her as she left. "See you at home."

Grandpa Busto had seen us drive up and came out to greet us. He had other plans.

"I'd like to show you our garden," he began as Annie drove off. It dawned on me that I wouldn't be ten minutes behind Annie, but it didn't matter. We walked through the garage where he stopped to show me his Boeing memorabilia. He had spent almost forty years working for the Boeing Company. (I had just completed ten years on the Boeing payroll at that time, so I had a ways to go.)

When we walked through the garage and out into the backyard, I was amazed at the huge garden. These folks had obviously mastered the skill of gardening: everything was hearty and I didn't see a single weed. I thought back to when I was a kid and had to spend many long summer afternoons weeding our garden, wondering why the weeds always grew twice as fast and tall as everything else. My dad was a stickler about weeds and wanted weed-free garden beds. I was always careless about pulling them, and it must have driven him nuts. He probably wanted to whack me with his hoe on more than one occasion.

We continued our garden tour; behind the garden stood a greenhouse loaded with all kinds of plants. Flowers bloomed everywhere—truly a gardener's paradise. Dad would have loved this place.

Grandma Busto hobbled out onto the deck and greeted me warmly. She used a walker to steady her steps and did a great job with it.

"I have some fresh lemonade and a plate of cookies for you

boys," she said smiling. "Come on up when you're ready."

"Ready?" I thought to myself. "She'll probably ask me to stay for supper and spend the night."

We gradually made our way through the rest of the backyard, then up the stairs and into the kitchen. A large pitcher of ice-cold lemonade and a plate of freshly baked cookies waited for us on the counter. We spent the next half hour talking about their children and ours, gardening, Boeing, and, yes, Oldsmobiles.

When it was time to go, these wonderful folks wanted to make sure I left with more than their prize Oldsmobile. We walked out to the driveway where they presented me with a sack of plums, a bag of potatoes, and a beautiful bouquet of dahlias for Annie. I bid them farewell and backed the blue Olds down their driveway for the very last time. I will always remember Grandpa and Grandma Busto standing there arm in arm, tears trickling down Grandma's cheek, while they waved a warm goodbye to me and their beloved Oldsmobile.

What I liked: Everything about the Bustos.

What I learned: Everyone has a story if we will only take the time to listen. It's always worth the investment.

25.

The Dirt Wagon

By the time Kevin and Mark were driving, it seemed the driveway was always full of cars. Most of their friends were driving their first cars, and I enjoyed talking with them about their "wheels." There is a special bond between a guy and his first car: who isn't proud to show off his car, especially when someone's dad asks about it? There was still one car memory I vowed to never share with them: I had painted my car with a paint brush, not once, but twice. The thought still makes me shudder. Some experiences just had to remain buried.

ISLAND GIVEAWAY

It was springtime and the earth was waking up after a long, wet Pacific Northwest winter. Kevin had finished high school and moved out, but Mark was still living at home and happened to be between VWs.

One afternoon a friend of Annie's called with a timely and unusual offer. These folks lived in Southern California and also owned a summer place in the San Juan Islands, located two hours north of Seattle via ferry. A state-owned ferry system shuttles cars and passengers between the islands and the mainland.

It turned out that these folks had an "island car" that they left by the ferry dock up on Lopez Island, one of the San Juan Islands. It provided them with transportation during visits to their island home. The offer? They were done with the car and wanted to give it to us for free. Such a deal!

Annie gratefully accepted the offer sight unseen. When I heard it was a Dodge Charger, I couldn't help but think of the wild car-chase in the movie *Bullitt*. In one scene, a Dodge Charger and a Mustang race around San Francisco, flying up and down and over the hills. Was I about to become the next Steve McQueen?

Reality came quickly, though, when we arrived on Lopez Island to bring the Charger home. This one was a brown 1984 two-door coupe with a couple of faded black factory-installed racing stripes on the sides. The only thing *Bullitt*-like on this baby was the cracked windshield that looked like someone took a shot at it. Though certainly no hot rod (or even a warm stick), it did seem like reliable enough transportation for the boys to use while their cars were out of commission. This island Charger was powered by a tired little four-cylinder engine mated with a four-speed transmission and had spent most of the past ten years parked by the ferry landing, waiting to shuttle its owners to their island getaway a few times each month. It had undoubtedly fit right in with the easygoing Lopez Island lifestyle. As the little car rattled along on the interstate during the ride home, I chuckled to myself about the prospects of this Charger joining our anything-but-laidback lifestyle. It was clear that this car would never make it to Daytona. I would be glad to just make it back to my driveway.

Mark was thrilled to have a semi-dependable car at his disposal and appreciated the use of the Charger. He was continuing to work over the '66 VW van and used the Charger (naming it the Dirt Wagon) as his daily driver during the initial rebuild process on the van. The little car proved to be fairly reliable for almost two years, providing some basic (can we say cheap?) transportation for the boys before it finally died in our driveway.

HEY, BRIAN!

The price to fix the Charger was going to be major. With Mark's VW van up and running, we decided to donate the Dirt Wagon to a company that picked up old cars and sold them for scrap. This time we didn't use the company that had hauled away the White Tornado several years before.

It was a bright and sunny Saturday afternoon when a driver with a big flatbed truck showed up to haul the Charger away to its final resting place. Already strapped onto the flatbed was an ancient Buick that looked as if it had been out to pasture for some time: it was covered in a layer of grime, with mud and grass packed up in the wheel wells. The Buick and the Charger would soon be hobbling off together.

As the junk man prepared to tow away the Charger, I noticed that our neighbor, Brian, had just finished hosing down his driveway with his big fancy pressure washer. Brian was a great neighbor and always seemed to have all the latest tools and equipment to keep his place looking sharp. Though he hadn't said anything, I knew that he didn't think much of our Dirt Wagon (complete with flat tire) parked on the street for the past several weeks. There was no way in the free world that Brian would have a dead anything parked in front of his house. Although he liked things shipshape around his place, Brian had a wicked sense of humor and loved to play practical jokes. That gave me an idea. Here was my chance.

"Hey, Brian!" I called, walking over to his driveway.

"What's up?" Brian asked, looking up cautiously as he carefully rolled up his pressure-washer hose.

"Hey," I continued enthusiastically, pointing to the tired old Buick. "Look what I just bought for 25 bucks! A great parts car!"

Brian looked as if he had just been slapped. His mouth was moving but no words were coming out. He finally mumbled a feeble, "Oh."

"Only kidding!" I said smiling as I burst out laughing.

Brian offered a nervous laugh and even smiled a little as I told him the real story. I was reasonably certain that if it were still hooked up, he would have turned the pressure washer on me at this point.

The Charger was soon hitched behind the truck, with the Buick secured on the flatbed, and together they slipped silently out of the neighborhood for their final ride. These old timers had probably logged more than 300,000 miles between them, and there must have been thousands of silent memories stashed away beneath their weather-beaten shells and woven into their worn upholstery. I solemnly watched them disappear around the corner. Etched in the Charger's dusty back window was an appropriate epitaph: "I'm soooo tired."

What I liked: The price.

What I learned: Not all Chargers were created equal.

26.

Tiggerific!

It was 1999 and while many folks were wondering about the pending Y2K challenge and how to adjust, I found myself wondering about another truck and how to adjust. Babe the Blue Olds was still a real beauty, but I missed the all-around utility of a pickup truck. The first Toyota pickup had served us well, so we started looking for another one.

Our search led us to a 1989 Toyota 4x4 SR5 extended cab pickup. The original owner, who had meticulously cared for it since new, was selling this ten-year-old prize. The owner's garage was so clean and tidy you could serve lunch off the floor. This truck was dark metallic gray, the same color as the 1988 model that Mark had picked out years before. It also had oversized tires and fancy wheels that really dressed it up. Another bonus was the SR5 package that included all the options the first Toyota lacked, including bucket seats, tilt wheel, and cruise control. The owner had even installed an upgraded stereo with an amplifier and extra speakers. Sweet deal! The four-cylinder engine boasted decent gas mileage to boot. It was sort of like love at first sight (okay, maybe not exactly like when I first laid eyes on Annie—or the '84 Cutlass Coupe). I did my homework and discovered that the '89 Toyota SR5 had won the prestigious Truck of the Year award by *Motor Trend* magazine, which only fueled my interest in having this one parked in my garage. To my great surprise, Annie purchased it for me for our twenty-fifth wedding anniversary. My sweetheart! Although I was excited enough to flip cartwheels across the front lawn again, I knew at this point in my life I would have probably wound up with an injury, so I refrained.

Now that we had firmly established the tradition of naming the cars in our fleet, it was time to play "name that truck." Our daughter, Kristen, decided that it should be named Tigger after a favorite Disney character. The name stuck, and it wasn't long before I placed a small stuffed Tigger on the dashboard. He has remained there ever since! At the time we also owned a blue 1993 Toyota 4-Runner named Torey. Torey and Tigger soon became household names.

Although I loved Tigger, it was hard to let go of Babe the Blue Olds Cutlass. I couldn't have my cake and eat it too (though I sure thought about it), so we put a For Sale sign in Babe's window and parked it along the street. Bingo. It didn't take long at all to find a new home for Babe, and I felt good about the sale: The buyer was an older man who loved Oldsmobiles almost as much as I did. That helped a lot, but I did feel bad when Babe backed out of our driveway for the last time. I knew then how the Bustos must have felt a few years earlier when they, too, waved goodbye.

Our new little truck had arrived with only a couple of minor flaws. There was a small dent down low on the right rear quarter panel, and the bed/box didn't hold a shine very well. Not a problem at all, but after a couple of years of trying all kinds of cleaner waxes, we decided to have the dent taken out and the box repainted. This would involve removing the standard silver Toyota decals that ran down the sides of the truck and the SR5 decal on the tailgate. But once the project had started, the body shop technician called to tell me that the identical Toyota decals were not available as the truck was already over twelve years old. The "fix" turned out to be a great one.

The body shop applied the estimated cost of the new decals to more paint and wound up painting both sides of the truck from bumper to bumper. Once that was completed they put me in touch with an auto detailer who specialized in custom pin-striping and decal work. He provided me with a catalog full of ideas, and we settled on a custom set of blue and gray decals to dress up the sides and tailgate. Tigger looked brand new and definitely set apart from all the rest. With over 120,000 miles logged on the odometer, this head turner of its own kind was humming along like a well-oiled machine.

SIXTEEN TONS AND WHAT DO YOU GET

One of our home-improvement projects involved pouring a slab of concrete in preparation for a hot tub. After researching the cost of having the concrete delivered, I decided to haul it myself. I thought I was doing the right thing, but in reality, I should have asked a few more questions before diving in.

The plan was to purchase a yard of concrete, which came in a small trailer (basically a box on wheels). The cement was mixed at the concrete store and then loaded on the trailer. And in case you are wondering (as I should have at the time), there was no paddle in the box to stir the concrete en route to the project. Timing is everything, as this do-it-yourselfer soon found out.

The Toyota efficiently pulled this load of concrete until we came to the long, steep hill between the cement store and my backyard, the site of our future hot tub. As I proceeded up the hill, I started to smell "fried clutch," not to be mistaken for fried chicken. By the time we reached the top of the hill, Tigger was groaning, and as we barreled down the other side, the fried clutch smell now mingled with the telltale aroma of fried brakes. There must be a scientific law out there somewhere that addresses the thrust that a load of concrete adds to a vehicle when headed down a steep hill. We did make it into the backyard, where I was about to learn one of the laws of physics. This came to light when I realized I needed to back up not only across the newly seeded lawn but also uphill. Tigger's four-wheel drive helped a lot (and I tried ever so carefully not to spin the tires), but this process really took its toll on the clutch. Ah . . . the aroma of fried clutch, hot brakes, and fresh concrete.

By the time I was almost there, it was apparent that I would have to use a wheelbarrow to move the concrete to the hot tub pad area. A wheelbarrow full of concrete is heavy enough to maneuver by itself, so I was glad to see our oldest son, Kevin, arriving to assist with the project. Between us we emptied the trailer and spread nearly the entire first load, but it became clear that we'd need a second yard of concrete to finish the task. The clutch and brakes had cooled off (at least I couldn't smell them!), so I decided to try again and go for load number two. Tigger ran fine with the empty trailer in tow, which helped me keep my wits about me. For incentive, I kept picturing myself one day lounging in the hot tub with Annie, sipping a cool drink, with warm water swirling around us.

In less than half an hour I was again on my way home with the second helping of concrete. Tigger had decided to play hardball within a mile of the concrete store and wouldn't even cooperate on the level, not to mention on any hills that would be involved in the trek back home. Anyone who has worked with concrete knows that time is of the essence and that the concrete in the paddleless trailer is not going to necessarily wait to get poured before it decides to set up. Duh! I parked the truck and sprinted back to the concrete store for help.

The burly man behind the counter was Mr. Concrete himself, and he offered to assist when he heard of my predicament. We jumped into his big Ford pickup to retrieve the trailer of hardening concrete. He was kind enough not to scold me for towing a yard of concrete with a four-cylinder Toyota, especially up a steep hill. The big Ford loomed over the Toyota, which could have fit into the bed of the Ford with room to spare. We hooked up the trailer of concrete to the Ford and pulled into our backyard just minutes later.

Mr. Concrete wasn't the least bit concerned about my newly seeded backyard, but the same laws of physics were still in place when the big Ford tried to push the load of concrete up the hill to the hot tub site, backward no less. We wound up with two long ruts through the backyard and mud splattered everywhere.

With Kevin's help we unloaded the second trailer and spread the concrete, completing the job. Mr. Concrete had no sooner pulled out of the driveway when Annie pulled in. I guess I forgot to mention it was cement-pouring day, so you can imagine her comments as she surveyed the backyard disaster. Had it been midsummer, I might have been banished to the doghouse for the night, but it was well into September and plenty chilly at night. Annie mercifully concluded that I had experienced enough pain that day and said no more about it.

When the new hot tub was delivered, the very efficient delivery man was quick to point out that the slab we had poured was at least two inches thicker than it needed to be.

"Now he tells me," I mumbled to myself, knowing that I should have asked a lot more questions before jumping into the concrete project. I tried to smile and thanked him for this piece of valuable information, but secretly I couldn't wait for him to get off my property before he had a chance to tell Annie. In the end, we were all pleased with the hot tub project, complete with a gazebo, a skylight, landscaping, yard lights, and Tiki lamps.

I ended up replacing Tigger's clutch and brakes, which only served to drive up the ultimate cost of the hot tub. I'm happy to report that, five years later, Annie and I are still spending many relaxing evenings out in the swirling waters of our hot tub, Tiki lamps glowing all around us, just like I pictured back when all we had was a slab of concrete. That freshly seeded grass recovered and eventually grew into an attractive lawn, and whenever I sweep the patio I see the words Kevin carved in the wet concrete that chilly autumn day: Bell Family 2002.

What I liked: Tigger is alive and well at more than 230,000 miles.

What I learned: A yard of concrete weighs over 2,000 pounds.

27.

Bumper to Bumper

Of all the vehicles that have come and gone in my life, one is different from all the rest: while all of my cars have served me, this unique vehicle exists to serve others—from crime victims and families burned out of their homes to police officers and firefighters at the scene of an emergency.

This vehicle, called Support 7, is a customized twenty-six-foot motor home complete with emergency lights and housed in our local fire station. This unit is totally outfitted with a generator, bathroom and shower facilities, and essential food and supplies needed in any emergency situation. It's designed to provide privacy, shelter, and basic needs for anyone facing a crisis. The back of the coach (where the bed would typically be in a motor home) has been reconfigured into an L shape sofa with a table. This area provides a warm, dry, and quiet place of genuine security for families to pull together during those critical initial hours following a tragedy. In the twenty-six feet between the front and rear bumpers of Support 7, I have seen lives changed, hearts touched, and needs met as we've been there to serve others in their time of need.

Support 7 is an extension of the International Fire and Law Enforcement Chaplain's Ministry (ICM), a nonprofit organization founded by my friend Ken Gaydos. It began with a vision that Ken had more than twenty years ago while serving as chaplain for the Edmonds Fire Department. As chaplain, Ken accompanied the fire department on their calls—day and night. One cold winter night they rolled up to the scene of a house fully engulfed in flames. Ken says he'll never forget the sight of the shocked family who had escaped the inferno: there they stood huddled under a single blanket, shivering in the night with nowhere to go. Ken knew they needed a place to get warm, away from the noise and chaos. On another occasion, an anxious family had gathered on the beach with nowhere to go while divers searched for their child, who hadn't returned from a diving expedition.

The Support 7 coach is staffed 24/7 by a team of trained volunteers who serve on the scene alongside local fire and law enforcement personnel, providing shelter and light refreshments for family members and emergency services personnel. A family in a crisis situation can gather here, away from insensitive onlookers and media lenses. The local fire and law enforcement agencies fully endorse the Support 7 team and partner with them in emergency situations, allowing these agencies to focus on the fire or emergency situation while the Support 7 Team helps the family members impacted by the emergency.

In the five years I've served as a Support 7 volunteer, I've seen some incredible situations unfold while "on scene." One freezing winter night we were dispatched to a house fire. The long driveway that led down to the house was a sheet of ice. We had no sooner parked the Support 7 coach at the top of the driveway when a young couple appeared, barefoot and in their pajamas, wrapped in a piece (and not a very big piece) of carpet padding. We settled them inside the warm coach, wrapped them in clean blankets, and poured them mugs of hot chocolate. They expressed gratitude for the warm, secure place to wait for relatives who lived on the other side of town to come and pick them up.

In another event, a tanker truck crashed and caught fire on the interstate near our suburban community north of Seattle. Amazingly, the driver escaped serious injury. Support 7 was dispatched to assist with rehab, refreshment, and on-scene comfort facilities for personnel from the various agencies that responded to the crisis, including fire crews from surrounding districts, city police and state patrol officers, Federal Emergency Management Agency (FEMA) reps, and numerous media reporters. The Boeing Company even dispatched a specially designed fire truck equipped with foam spray that was used to ultimately douse the flames. For well over twelve hours at the fiery crash scene, Support 7 volunteers served drinks and even cooked hot dogs for hungry personnel from the participating agencies. In addition, local restaurants, in partnership with Support 7, donated pizzas and fried chicken that we served as the hours ticked by. I never imagined that my volunteer job description would include serving dinner on the interstate expressway, but that's the nature of Support 7 work—doing whatever it takes to fill needs in a crisis.

In yet another house-fire tragedy, the family of an elderly gentleman who had perished in the blaze gathered in the coach to console one another. At times like that, Support 7 volunteers quietly go about the business of just being there to offer comfort and a shoulder.

What I've learned firsthand as a Support 7 volunteer is that tragedy can strike at any time—and when it does, the Support 7 team is ready. It might be a murder in a quiet residential neighborhood, a hostage-taking bank robbery, a drowning on a crowded beach, an airplane crash, or a house fire in the middle of the night. In all honesty, when a call awakens me at 2 a.m., I'm not eager to roll out of a nice, comfy bed and go out into the cold night. But knowing that I will be helping a family in crisis makes it all worthwhile. As a Support 7 volunteer, I've witnessed just about every emotion imaginable shared inside the Support 7 coach, as families get close and respond to one another in their time of deepest need. Knowing that we can assist by providing them that quiet place during their time of crisis warms my heart every time.

As I reflect on our team of Support 7 volunteers, I'm reminded of what a diverse bunch we are. Several team members have retired from various professions; some of us still have our "day jobs" as teacher, bus driver, project manager, aerospace engineer, mechanic, car salesman, construction worker, draftsman, and business owner. I think all of the Support 7 volunteers would agree that "we make a living by what we do, we make a life by what we give." It's also true that "to the world, we might be just a small group of people. But to a small group of people, like a family in crisis, we are the world."

What I like: The opportunity to *be there* for someone in their time of deepest need.

What I learned: People don't care how much you know until they know how much you care.

28.

Reflections in the Rearview Mirror

As I look back at the cars in my life, my chromies, I have to say that it has been a wild and crazy but wonderful ride. As I have thought about the time and place that each vehicle has occupied in my life, the memories have flooded in. Sifting through old pictures, I've uncovered memories to treasure forever. And the best part is that this wonderful adventure is not over yet.

Our three kids have grown up, moved out, and left us with a much quieter house. There isn't a project-in-the-works parked alongside the garage. Our current fleet stands at two: Annie drives Tanna, the gray 2003 Toyota Corolla Sport, and I drive Tigger, the 1989 Toyota SR5 pickup, still going strong at well over 230,000 miles.

Someone recently asked me what my next car will be, and at least a half dozen new models—foreign and domestic—come to mind, any of which I would love to see in my garage. I still make it to the auto show each year to look them all over and maybe pick up a few brochures, just like I remember doing with my dad back in the fifties. Auto shows have changed a lot in fifty years!

In the used category, it would be a tough choice for sure, but my short list would include a '66 Ford Mustang (with an automatic transmission for Annie), an '84 Olds Cutlass Coupe, and maybe even a '57 Pontiac sedan like the one that got away. There are so many favorites, it would be hard to choose.

I've heard it said that "someday we will look back on all this and plow into a parked car." If that ever happens, I hope I'm driving the Pontiac.

Looking back over my assortment of chromies has unlocked memories—both heartwarming and bittersweet. My hope is that you, too, can pause to journey down memory lane and reconnect with your own band of chromies. It's definitely worth the trip. And it just might warm your heart the same way that my chromies have warmed mine, because Chrome Is Where the Heart Is.

MY CHROMIES

1.	'59 Chevy Impala	blue and white
2.	'59 Chevy Impala (the other one)	yellow, bright yellow, maroon (ugh!)
3.	'60 Pontiac Grand Safari wagon	turquoise and white
4.	'66 Ford Mustang	silver blue
5.	'69 Olds Vista Cruiser	avocado green with wood grain
6.	'66 Dodge Coronet	yellow
7.	'71 Ford Pinto	forest green
8.	'74 Ford Pinto Squire wagon	avocado green with wood grain
9.	'77 Ford Pinto wagon	silver
10.	'71 Ford LTD sedan	brown
11.	'68 Ford pickup and camper	powder blue and white
12.	'84 Honda Accord	silver blue
13.	'71 Mercury Marquis wagon	brown with wood grain
14.	'88 Toyota 4x4 pickup	gray
15.	'79 Buick Estate wagon	maroon
16.	'84 Olds Cutlass Coupe #1	gray with white landau roof
17.	'86 Chevy Caprice wagon	gold
18.	'84 Olds Cutlass Coupe #2	blue with dark blue landau roof
19.	'88 Toyota Camry	blue
20.	'67 Ford wagon (White Tornado)	white
21.	'95 Toyota 4-Runner (Belle)	black
22.	'84 Olds Cutlass sedan #3 (Betty)	black
23.	'84 Olds Cutlass Coupe #4 (Huck)	red (kind of)
24.	'84 Olds Cutlass Coupe #5 (Babe)	blue with dark blue landau roof
25.	'89 Toyota SR5 4x4 pickup (Tigger)	gray
26.	'91 Honda Accord (Rhonda)	maroon
27.	'93 Toyota 4-Runner (Torey)	marine blue
28.	'03 Toyota Corolla Sport (Tanna)	gray

ISBN 142513810-1

Edwards Brothers Malloy
Thorofare, NJ USA
May 2, 2016